ESSENTIAL ECONOMICS

For the IB Diploma and A level

ESSENTIAL ECONOMICS

For the IB Diploma and A level

Don Campbell LL.B (hons), BSc,

Dip Math, PGCE, Cert TESOL.

ISBN: 978-1-326-29883-8

PublishNation
www.publishnation.co.uk

CONTENTS

DEMAND

1. Demand sees the world from the standpoint of the consumer. Demand can be defined as the quantity demanded of a product at any given price. The demand for bread in a small Swiss village might be 500 loaves a day at an average price of 3 Swiss francs.

2. The law of demand states that if the price of a good or service falls, quantity demanded (QD) will rise, while an increase in price will lead to a decrease in quantity demanded. This is on the assumption that nothing else changes (ceteris paribus).

3. The normal demand curve is downward sloping, showing an inverse relationship between price and quantity demanded.

4. There is a crucial difference between demand and quantity demanded in Economics. It is important to realise that a change in price does not cause demand to change, it is only quantity demanded which alters. This is called a movement along a demand curve and is shown below.

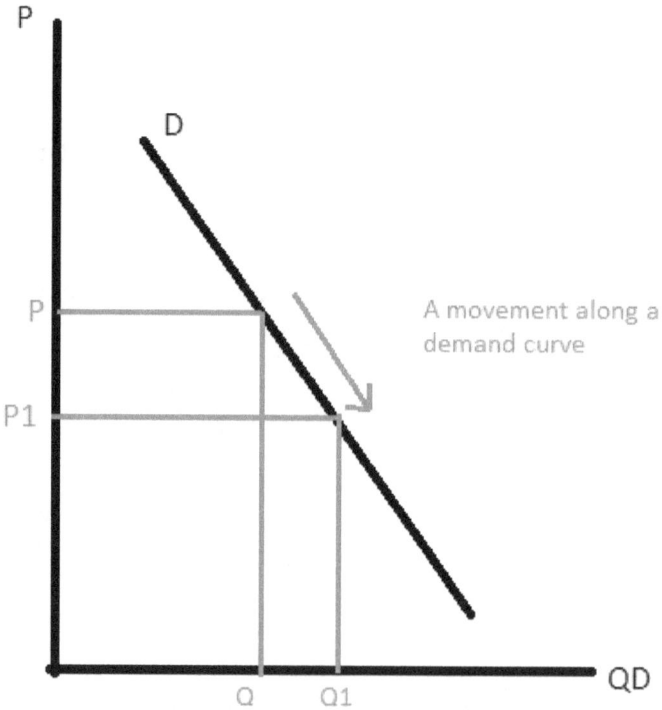

P

D

P

P1

A movement along a
demand curve

Q   Q1

QD

5. When demand changes, the whole demand curve shifts
to the right, showing an increase in demand, or to the
left, illustrating a fall in demand. This means that at
each price point there is a rise or fall in QD. A rise in
demand for bread might mean that at the same price of
3 Swiss francs, 600 loaves are sold rather than 500.
Changes in demand are caused by factors other than
the price of the product, for example economic growth
or recession, income levels, income tax, interest rates,
population, advertising, marketing, weather, taste and
preference, or the price of related substitute and
complementary products.

SHIFT OF A DEMAND CURVE

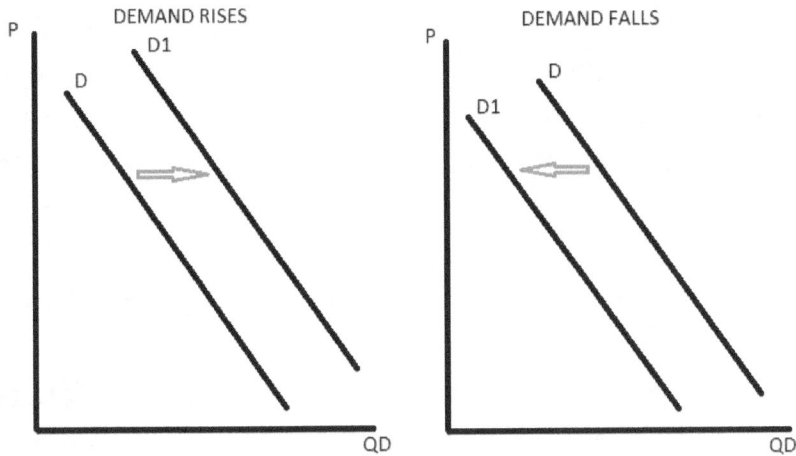

6. If there is strong economic growth, this implies rising incomes, falling unemployment, and increasing consumer confidence. This will be translated into rising demand for nearly all products, such as food, clothing, automobiles, computers and mobile phones. Similarly, falling interest rates result in a lower cost of borrowing and this will fuel demand. A cut in income tax would have the same impact, as disposable income rises. If there is a successful advertising campaign, this will stimulate demand for that product. One example is the success of Apple iPhones in China, due to the strong brand cachet. Hot weather will increase demand for products like bottled water, soft drinks and ice cream. The price of related products is particularly significant. If the price of a Samsung mobile phone rises, demand for the substitute Apple product would increase. If the

price of gasoline decreases, demand for the complementary product, automobiles, would rise.

7. Demand can also fall for many products if there is an economic recession. This is where gross domestic product (output) falls, and incomes decline on average. The fall in consumer confidence and job losses can cause a fall in demand for nearly all products, especially luxury items. Bad publicity can also seriously damage demand, for instance when mad cow disease ravaged demand for beef. If the government imposes high indirect tax on gin, demand for the complementary good, tonic, would tumble. A cut in the price of a Sony computer might trigger a decline in demand for the substitute Dell.

SUPPLY

1. Supply looks at the world from the viewpoint of the producer. Supply is defined as the quantity supplied of a product at any given price. The supply of oil might be 100 million barrels a day at a price of $60 a barrel. There is a direct relationship between price and the quantity supplied (QS). When the price rises, quantity supplied increases, while a fall in price causes QS to decline. The reason for this is that when the world price of a product like oil rises, this provides producers with an incentive to locate and extract more oil, due to increased profit potential. A price change causes quantity supplied to change, and this is called a movement along a supply curve.

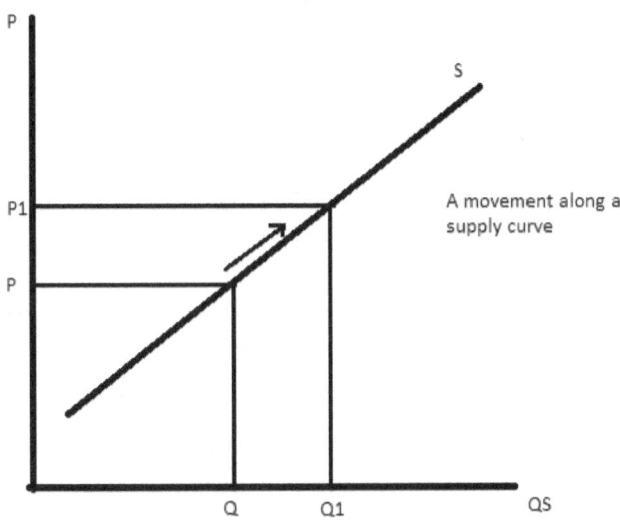

A movement along a supply curve

2. It is important to note that supply does not change when the world price alters, as the supply curve does not shift. When supply increases, the supply curve shifts to the right, while a fall in supply is shown by the supply curve shifting left. At each price there will be a rise or fall in QS. For example, if there is a fall in supply, at a price of $60, only 70 million barrels might be produced.   Changes in supply are caused by factors other than price, and the most important of these are average production costs, weather, indirect taxes and subsidies, geopolitics, the price of substitute producer goods, and matters concerning joint supply.

SHIFT OF A SUPPLY CURVE

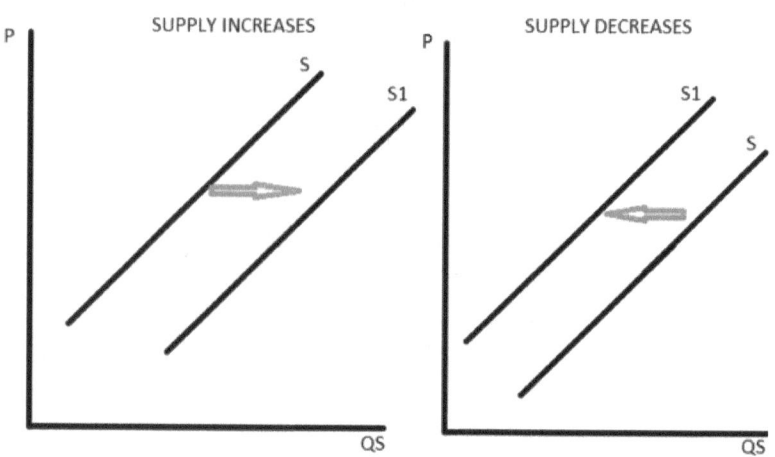

3. Weather has an important influence on the supply of products of agriculture and mining. A tornado in the Gulf of Mexico will disrupt world production of oil, causing supply to dwindle and the price to spike. Favourable weather can result in a bumper harvest of

products like pears or bananas. Geopolitical events such as war in the Middle East or an embargo on Russian exports can also effect supply of products like oil and gas. If the government increases indirect tax (tax on goods and services), this has the effect of cutting supply, because firms' costs effectively rise, as they have to pay the tax. A subsidy payment to a producer would have the opposite effect, causing supply to grow.

4. One of the most important influences on supply is the average cost of producing the product. Average cost means the cost of making one unit. If average cost falls, supply increases because firms are in a position to bring more of the product to the market for the same cost. If labour costs fall, or energy costs, or raw material costs, all of these factors will cause supply to rise, with the supply curve shifting to the right. New technology often cuts average costs, while high wage demands in excess of productivity have the opposite effect.

5. The price of substitute producer products can sometimes be important. If a beef farmer faces falling prices, he will have an incentive to consider switching to pig or poultry farming, resulting in a boost in the supply of these products.

6. Joint supply is where, for instance, the price of beef rises, causing QS to rise and as a side effect the supply of the jointly produced product, leather, increases.

EQUILIBRIUM PRICE

1. The point at which demand meets supply is the equilibrium price and quantity. This is also known in many markets as the spot price. The equilibrium in the crude oil market might be a price of $60 and a quantity of 100m barrels a day.

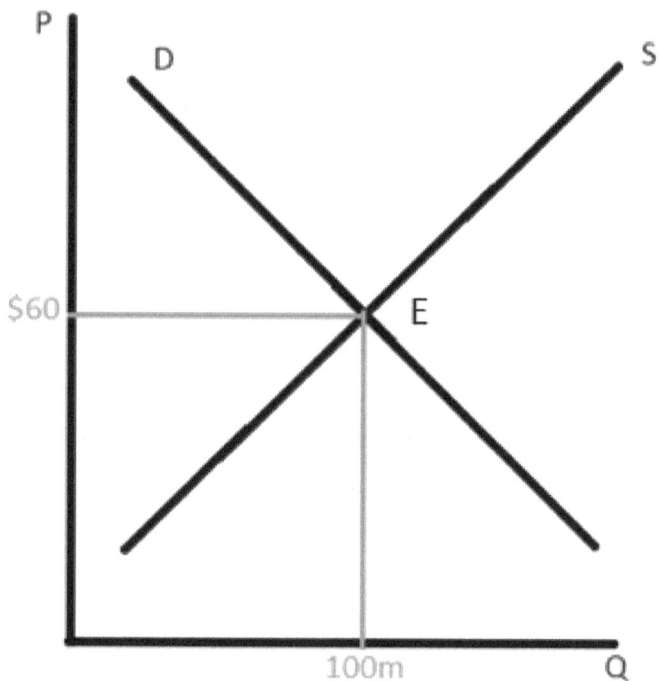

2. The demand and supply diagram allows us to explore the workings of the price mechanism; what the economist Adam Smith called "the invisible hand". We start with the equilibrium price and quantity, then external events will take place, which impact on the market for particular goods and services. Let us consider firstly the market for oil. A decision by OPEC to increase output quotas, will cause supply to rise, and this is shown by the supply curve shifting to the right. The effect might be a fall in price from $80 to $40 a barrel.

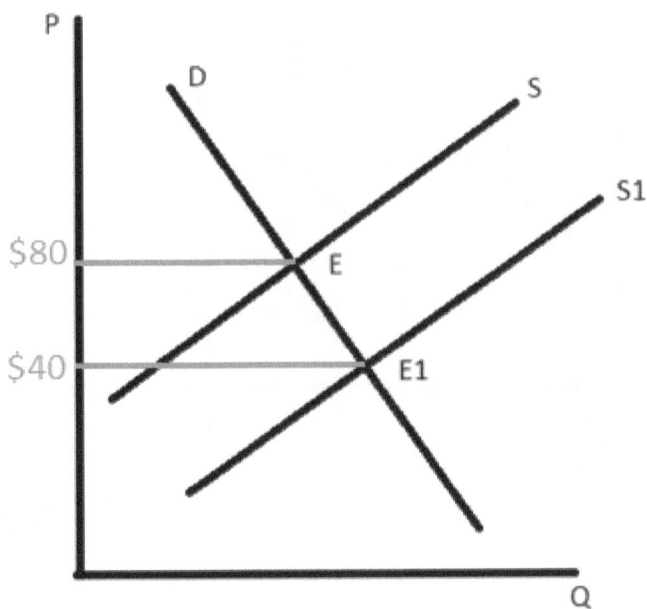

3. If there is a frost in Brazil, this will impact on the market for coffee, because the delicate coffee plants will perish, causing supply of coffee to decline, with the supply curve shifting to the left. A steep price rise would follow, perhaps compounded by a measure of panic buying boosting demand.

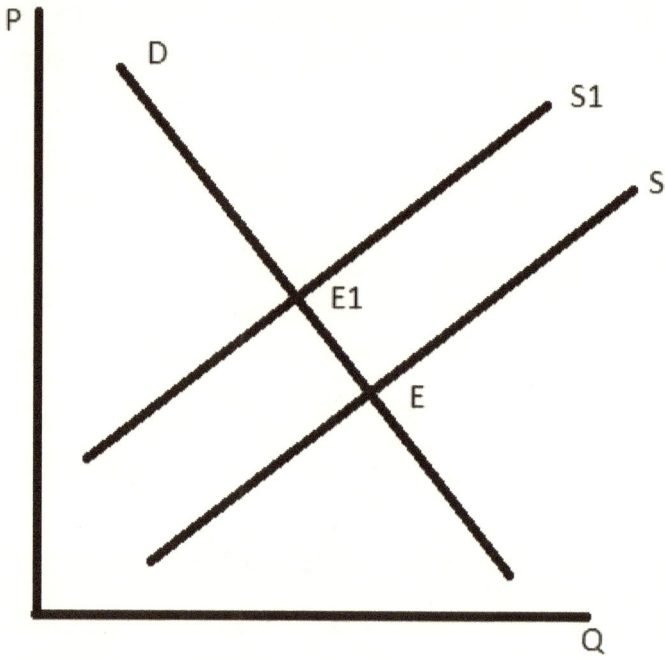

4. Botswana is a major diamond producer. The world recession in 2008, caused by the sub-prime crisis, resulted in demand for diamonds falling rapidly, due to rising unemployment and falling consumer confidence in developed economies. The demand curve shifts to the left, causing a steep fall in prices. In fact many diamond mines stopped production.

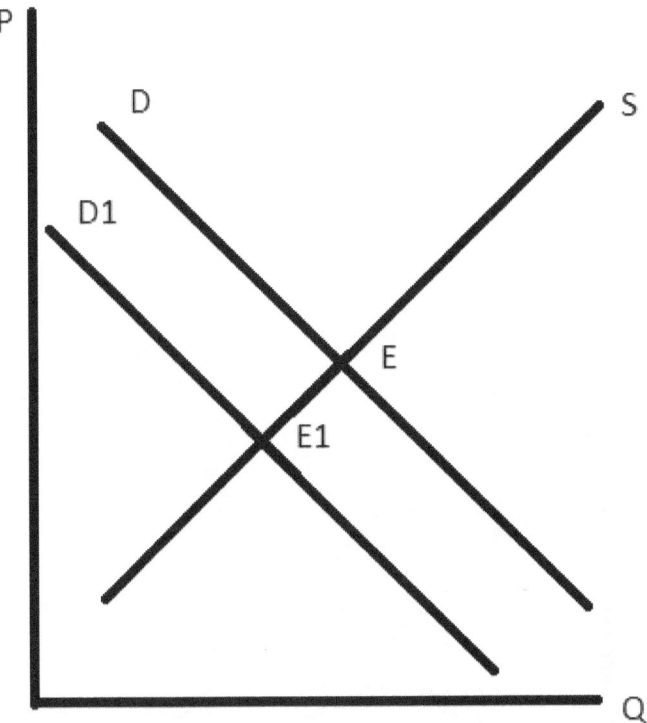

5. The Swiss watch industry has recently encountered a falling off of demand in China, where luxury gifting is now seen as politically incorrect. (The appreciation of the Swiss franc can best be modelled as a price rise causing QD to tumble). Clearly lower demand is bad for sales of luxury timepieces, causing a downward pressure on prices. Revenue is price multiplied by quantity, and export revenue will be damaged. Other names for revenue are income or turnover. The revenue box is shown on the next diagram. If revenue falls, profit, which is revenue minus costs, is also likely to decline.

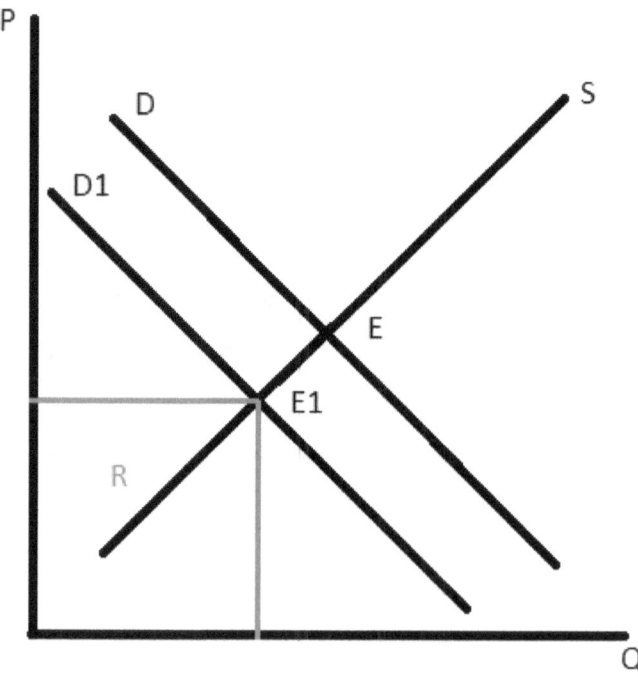

6. There has been a recent growth in demand for Apple iPhones in China, due to the perceived attractiveness of the brand. This is in spite of high prices, and much competition from domestic producers. The rise in demand due to this fashion trend causes the curve to shift to the right, improving revenue and profit.

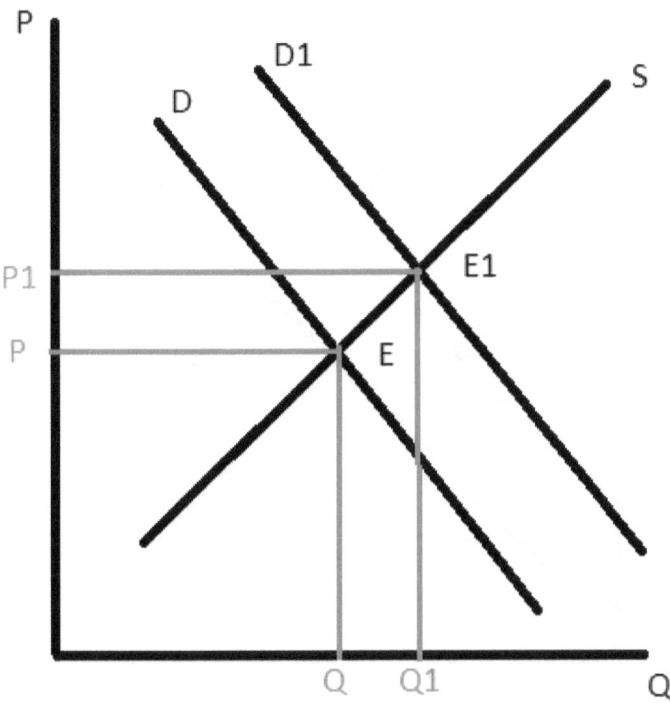

7. Many markets allow us to explore a more complicated combination of influences. The world market for copper is one such example. Tropical flooding can upset production in producer regions like Zambia, causing supply to decline, while slower growth rates in countries like China, or recession in the EU, can cause demand to dampen.

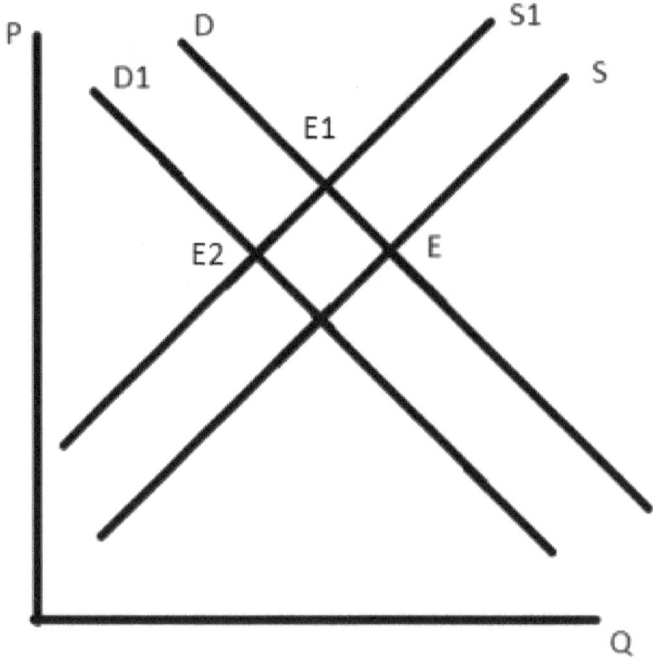

8. A computer maker might encounter falling production costs, due to a weakening of the oil price. This means that supply increases and the supply curve shifts to the right. Demand may increase due to economic recovery in the US and UK markets, shown by the demand curve shifting right.

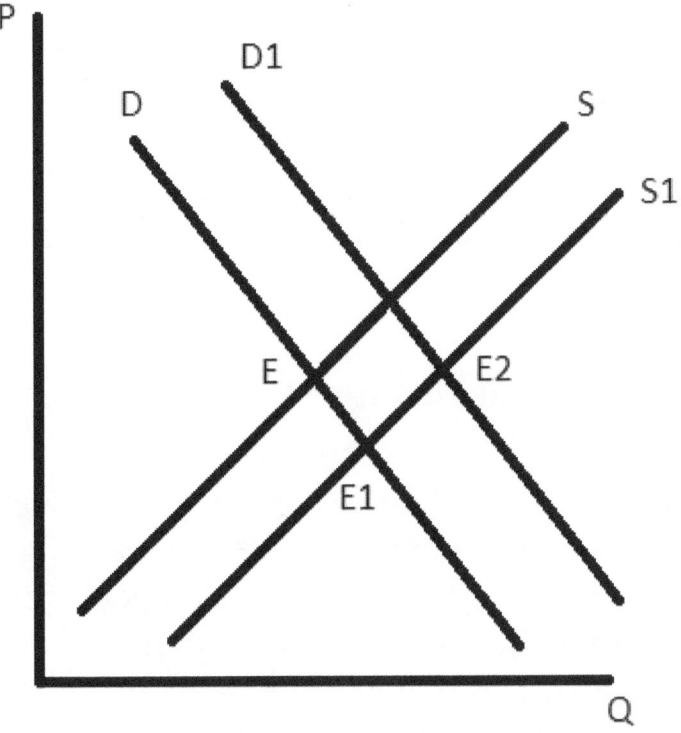

PRICE ELASTICITY OF DEMAND

1. One of the seminal thinkers on the topic of elasticity was Alfred Marshall, and his *Principles of Economics* (1890) dealt with some of these concepts.

2. Price elasticity of demand (PED) measures the responsiveness of quantity demanded to changes in price. At a practical level, a firm might change its price, and we can observe the effect on sales.

3. The formula for calculating PED is percentage change in quantity demanded, divided by percentage change in price.

4. As a mathematical expression $PED = \dfrac{\%\Delta\ QD}{\%\Delta\ P}$

5. Goods and services can be defined as being either elastic or inelastic in terms of PED, depending on the numerical value of their elasticity. If a good has a PED of more than 1, it is elastic, while a PED greater than zero and less than one is inelastic. It should be noted that all PED figures are actually negative, but the sign is usually ignored. The negative value comes from the fact that a price increase usually causes a fall in quantity demanded, and we are dividing a negative by a positive, giving a negative result.

6. In order to understand price elasticity of demand, it is essential to examine some real life examples. Consider the market for cigarettes. If the price rises by 5%, this may cause sales to fall by 1%. Using the formula above, we divide the 1% by the 5%. This means that the PED is 0.2. This figure is between zero and one, defining tobacco as an inelastic good. This means that for a 1% increase in price, quantity demanded will fall by less than 1%. Tobacco is inelastic because it is highly addictive. Even when the price rises sharply, often due to government indirect taxes, sales will fall by a far smaller amount. On a diagram, the inelastic market for cigarettes is shown as follows. (Note the steep gradient).

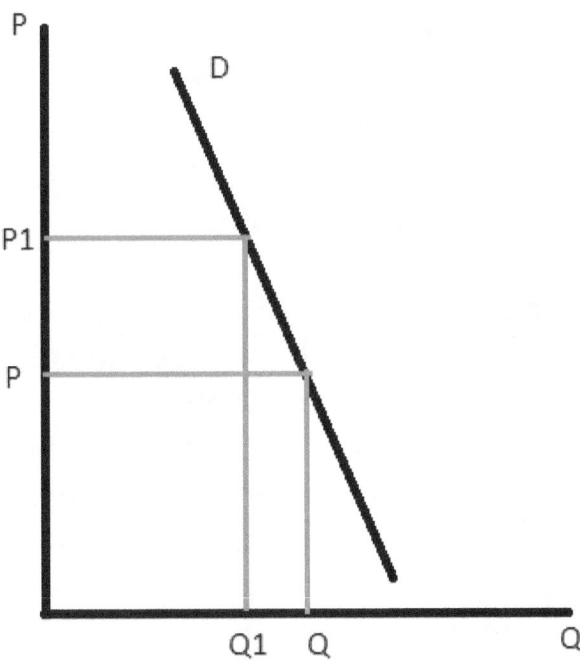

7. Goods and services are inelastic if they have few or no substitutes, if they are necessities, if they are general products, if they consume a small percentage of income, if purchase cannot be delayed or if they are addictive.

8. Formula milk is inelastic because it is essential for babies, there are no substitutes, if mother's milk is unavailable. Also, purchase cannot be delayed; the baby requires feeding now! Oil has precious few substitutes, making it highly inelastic. If you want to drive your car you need to fill it with gasoline; the purchase can't be delayed. Gold and diamonds are required by jewellers and have few real substitutes. Wheat is required to make bread. Alcohol and drugs are inelastic due to their highly addictive nature. The more general the product, the more it tends to be inelastic, so beef or chicken are more inelastic than a particular brand or packaged meal. If the purchase consumes a small part of income, such as a stamp or a newspaper or bread, it will often be inelastic.

9. Branded products, where there are many substitutes, are elastic in PED. In the local supermarket, there are many competing brands of orange juice and cereal, each of which is facing an elastic market with lots of competition. The markets for computers and automobiles have many substitutes, so that while we may have a preference for say a Renault, a Ford would ultimately suffice. The appropriate diagram is shown below, showing an elasticity of 3 on this occasion, as we

divide the percentage change in QD of 30% by the percentage change in price of 10%. (Note the non-steep gradient).

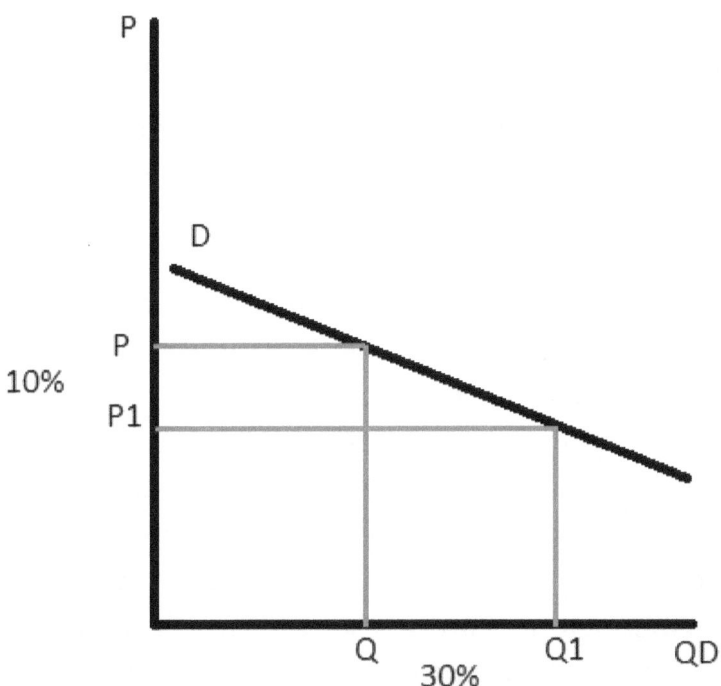

10. Price elasticity of demand is important because if a product is inelastic, and this can often be ascertained through market research, the firm can put up the price of its product and revenue will increase. The reason for this is a that with an inelastic good, a 1% rise in price will cause sales to fall by less than 1%, so revenue will increase. When the price is put up, quantity demanded will actually fall, so the firm's costs will tend to shrink. This means that the price hike will also increase profit.

11. The situation for an elastic product is not quite so clear. If a firm's product has a PED of say 2, putting the price up would obviously not be a good idea, because a 1% price rise would cause a drop in sales of 2%, and income would fall. Firms in an elastic market should consider reducing their prices to boost revenue and profit. If the firm cuts its price, quantity demanded will increase by a larger percentage. For example, a product with a PED of 2.5 will see sales rise by 2.5% if the price is cut by 1%. This means that revenue will rise. However, it is important to realise that extra sales will generate extra costs, as more of the product has to be produced and sold, so the price cutting strategy should only be employed if the extra revenue is more than the extra costs. Only in this situation will the extra revenue translate into extra profit. Another problem is that cost cutting in a market where there are only a small number of competing firms, who can observe each other's behaviour, can introduce the threat of a price war, from which every firm might lose.

12. There are some technical points to note on the topic of PED. A straight line demand curve actually does not have constant elasticity. On the diagonal curve below, the top part of the curve is elastic, while the bottom is inelastic. This reflects the fact that consumers are less price sensitive at low prices. The point mid curve has an elasticity of 1; unitary elasticity. We can check this by calculation. At the bottom of the curve, if the price increases from 1 to 2, causing QD to fall from 5 to 4, this is a 20% fall in QD caused by a 100% rise in price,

which is a PED of 0.2, which is inelastic. At the top of the curve, a price rise from 4 to 5 causes a fall in QD from 2 to 1. The percentage fall in QD is 50%, and the price rise is 25%, resulting in a PED of 2 which is elastic. This observation does not alter the fact that inelastic curves have a steep gradient, and elastic curves have a shallow gradient.

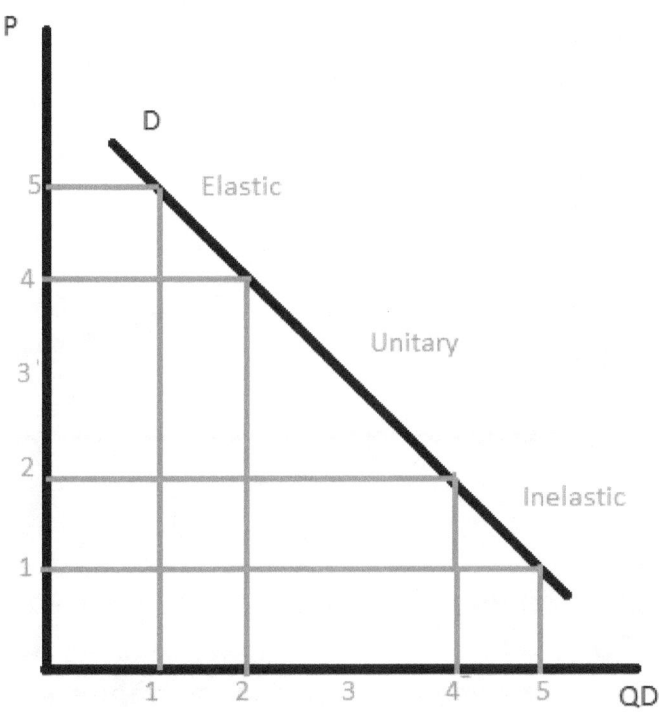

13. A demand curve with constant elasticity of 1 would look like this.

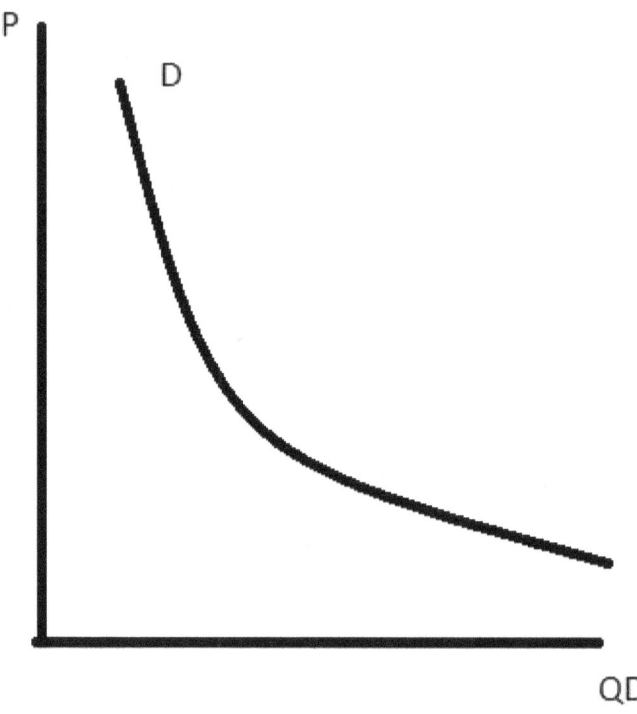

14. Theoretical limits arise when the PED is zero or infinity. Zero PED would arise when QD stays the same, irrespective of price changes, while infinite PED would be a situation where a tiny price increase causes sales to drop to zero. While these curves are unlikely to be much encountered in real life, a person in need of a life-saving drug, might pay virtually any price, making the PED virtually zero. Someone lost in the desert, in need of water, might face a similarly inelastic curve. A

near infinite curve might be encountered when two sellers are selling the same product in the same location, but one of them decides to charge a much higher price. Most consumers would migrate to the lower price.

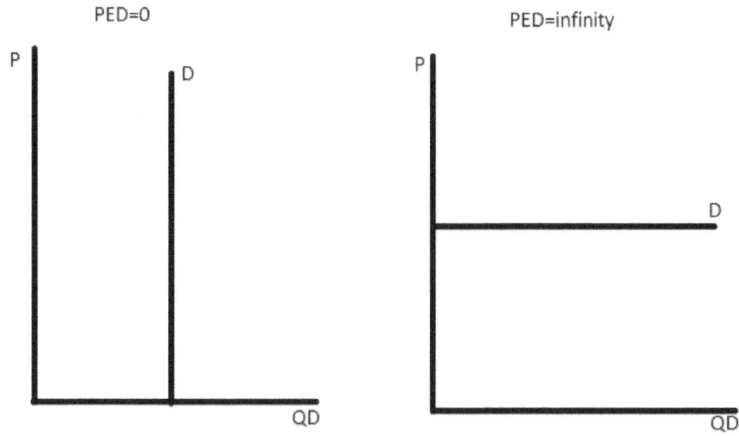

PRICE ELASTICITY OF SUPPLY

1. Price elasticity of supply (PES) looks at the world of price elasticity from the standpoint of the producer, while PED is viewed from the standpoint of the consumer.

2. PES measures the responsiveness of quantity supplied to changes in market price. The formula is percentage change in quantity supplied divided by percentage change in price.

3. $PES = \dfrac{\%\Delta\ QS}{\%\Delta\ P}$

4. If the PES is greater than 1, a product is elastic in terms of price elasticity of supply, while a PES of greater than zero and less than one is inelastic. So PES is a sort of mirror image of PED.

5. Most primary commodities, by which we mean products of farming, fishing, forestry and mining, are inelastic in terms of price elasticity of supply. This means that a 1% change in world price will result in less than a 1% change in quantity supplied. The reason for this is that agricultural products take a growing season to produce, so a rise in market price will have little immediate effect on QS. Similarly, minerals are usually very capital intensive to locate and extract, and there is

no swift response to a price stimulus. Locating and extracting new supplies of crude oil can be extremely expensive and time consuming. The inelastic PES of primary goods is seen below. (Note the steep gradient).

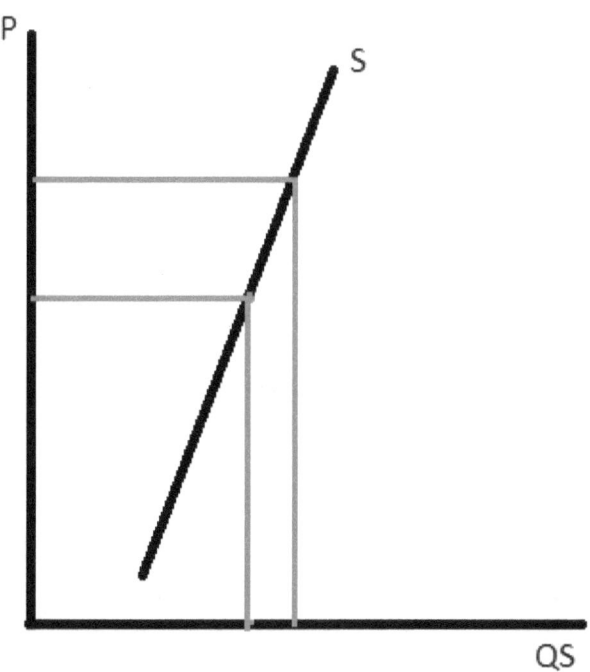

6. In contrast to primary goods like oil, gold, copper, wheat, apples, grapes, coffee, timber and cod, secondary products, which are manufactured, tend to be much more elastic in price elasticity of supply. Thus, products like computers, automobiles, clothing, pencils, carpets, furniture, books, soft drinks and packaged meals, are often elastic in supply. This means that a small price increase on the market, due to higher

demand, will generate a larger increase in quantity supplied. Factories will simply employ more workers, on more frequent shifts, running machinery to capacity for longer hours, to take advantage of the profit potential from rising prices.

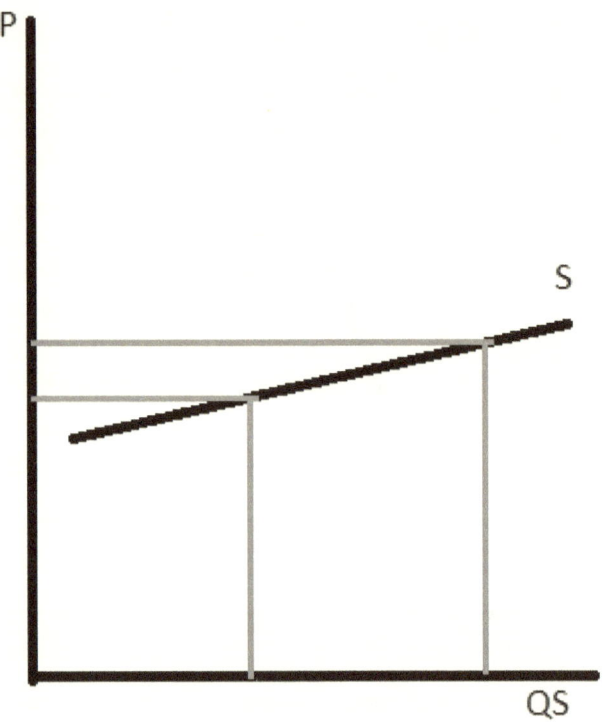

7. Also, when prices on the world market fall, manufacturing firms can cut output rapidly, laying off excess workers. However a farmer has no such option; the crop planted will turn to harvest in several months, and he cannot change the level of output in the face of dropping prices.

8. Service industries like tourism, banking or education have an elasticity of supply which lies somewhere between primary goods and secondary goods. The service sector is called the tertiary sector. It is possible to cut back on staff in response to falling prices, due to lack of demand, but it will usually take some time. A teacher can be employed for fewer hours, but it can take a year for the new contract to take effect. Casual workers in tourism can be laid off more readily, as they often have short term contracts.

INCOME ELASTICITY OF DEMAND

1. Consumers' incomes rise during periods of economic growth and fall during a recession. Income elasticity of demand measures the responsiveness of QD to changes in income. The formula is percentage change in QD divided by percentage change in income.

2. YED=$\dfrac{\%\Delta\ QD}{\%\Delta\ I}$ (Y=yield or income)

3. Income elasticity looks at the effect of changing incomes on "the pattern of demand". Specifically, income elasticity divides the world into three categories of goods and services; inferior goods, normal goods, and superior goods. Inferior goods have a negative income elasticity, while normal goods have a positive income elasticity. Superior goods are a special type of normal goods, with an income elasticity greater than 1.

4. What does this mean in the real world? How can firms use this information to enhance profit? The key idea is that when incomes rise, demand increases for all normal goods, but especially for superior goods. When incomes rise, demand for so called inferior goods falls. Let us now consider a range of examples to illustrate this concept.

5. If there is strong economic growth, this leads to rising consumer confidence and increased income levels. Not surprisingly this is reflected in rising demand for normal goods like clothing and food. This is illustrated in the following diagram.

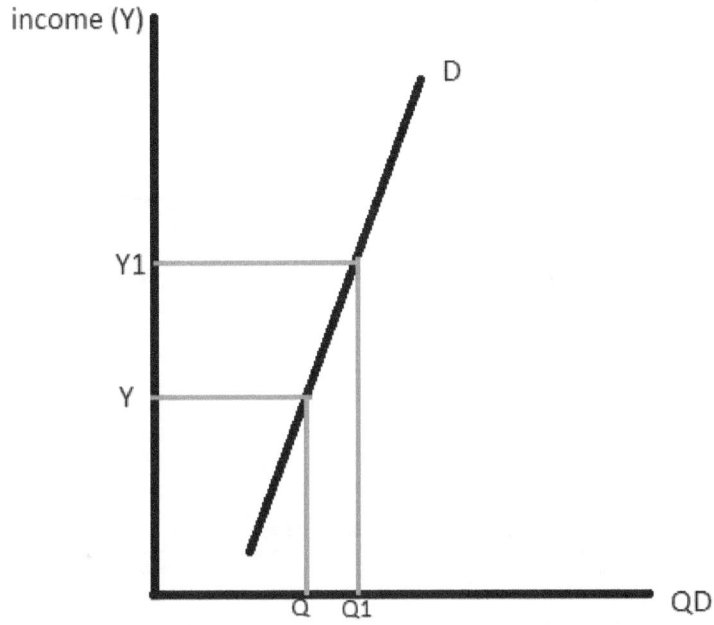

6. Of special interest is the case of luxury goods, such as expensive foreign vacations, designer clothing and Rolex watches. With these products, consumers respond to the economic "good times" by purchasing luxury products which they often cannot really afford. During periods of economic growth and prosperity, the demand for these superior goods rises fast. A small increase in incomes will often be reflected in massive purchases. We see in the following diagram that a 10%

growth rate in China, causes a 30% increase in spending on superior, luxury goods, illustrating a YED of 3.

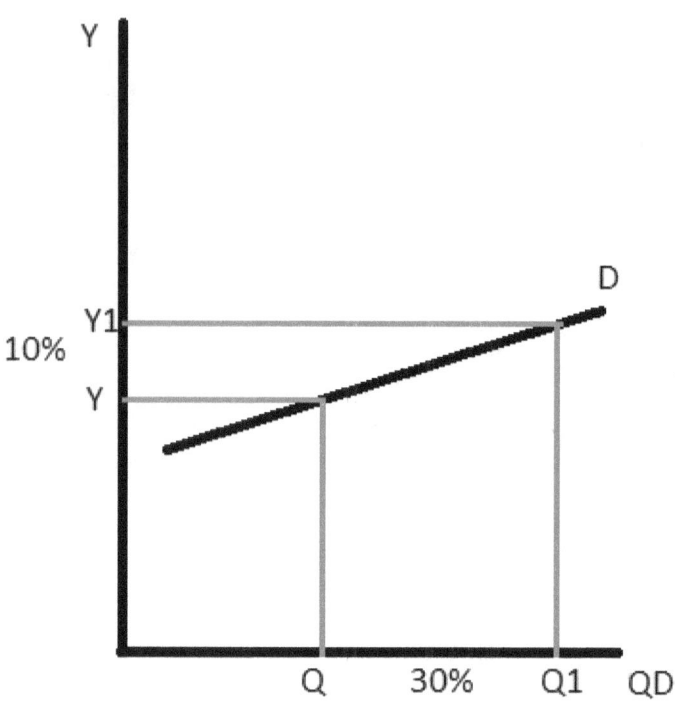

7. Inferior goods are also of great significance. These are products where demand falls as incomes rise. This is due to the fact that rising incomes and falling unemployment, causes an outburst of consumer optimism. Consumers think the good times will go on for ever, and they switch from lower quality, lower price products, to more extravagant goods and services. A family may switch from a value-for-money brand like McDonald's to a more costly Italian or Thai restaurant. It is important to note that the word

"inferior" is a relative term; what is inferior to one person in one context, may be normal or even superior to another person in a different context. To a starving person, a potato would not be an inferior good! Some foodstuffs are seen as being luxurious in some cultures, for example king prawns, but in the context of some religions this would be seen as an undesirable product. We see from the inferior goods diagram that demand falls as income rises.

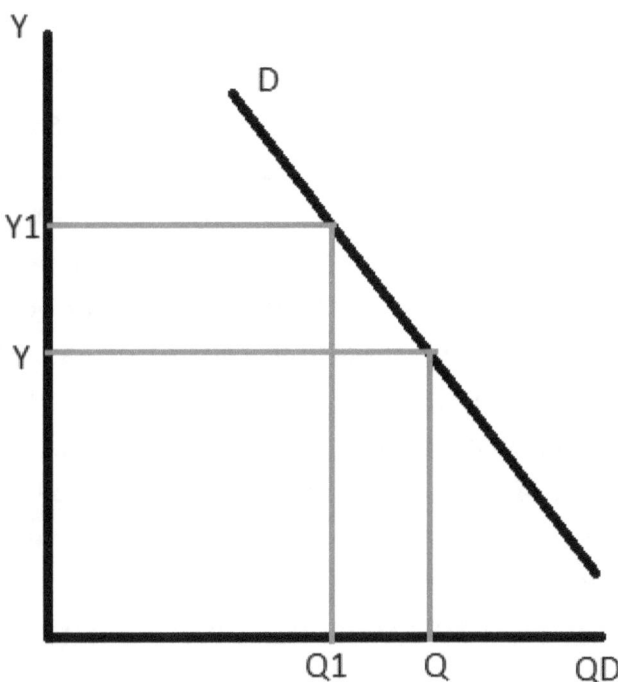

8. We can now discuss the business use of income elasticity. If there is strong economic growth in a country, that makes it a good target market for luxury

products. It is no accident that many Swiss, Italian and French luxury outlets are being opened in locales such as Beijing. There is perhaps little better place to sell an Hublot watch! There are interesting video clips available online, showing the chief executive of Hublot explaining the logic of opening outlets in fast growing economies. When the 2008 downturn impacted on the EU and the US, China and the Middle East provided an escape route for the luxury brand sellers.

9. In times of recession, when consumer confidence has taken a bash, this provides an opportunity for the enhanced sale of so called inferior goods. Sales of fast food expanded during the post 2008 recession, with some fast food companies posting record profits. This is because workers are cautious and have low "animal spirits" when the broader economy is in trouble. "Animal spirits" is a term coined by the celebrated economist Keynes, meaning the same as consumer confidence. Much consumer response is slightly irrational, and can be referred to as an irrational lack of exuberance. A climate of fear arises from bad publicity about the economy, and this is reflected in the lunchtime purchase of two hamburgers at 100 yen apiece, rather than a slap up meal in a posh restaurant.

CROSS ELASTICITY OF DEMAND

1. Cross elasticity of demand (CED) measures the responsiveness of quantity demanded of product B to a change in the price of product A. The formula is percentage change in QD of product B, divided by percentage change in price of product A.

2. $CED = \dfrac{\%\Delta\ QD\ good\ B}{\%\Delta\ P\ good\ A}$

3. CED sometimes called XED, especially concerns the relationship between close substitutes and complements. If two goods or services are close substitutes, they will have a high positive CED. Close complements have a high negative CED. We can illustrate this with the following examples.

4. Consider two petrol stations in the same small village. If one of the gas stations selects to raise its price by 5%, this may cause a lot of locals to transfer to the substitute gas station. The substitute may benefit from a 20% increase in trade, reflecting a CED of 4.

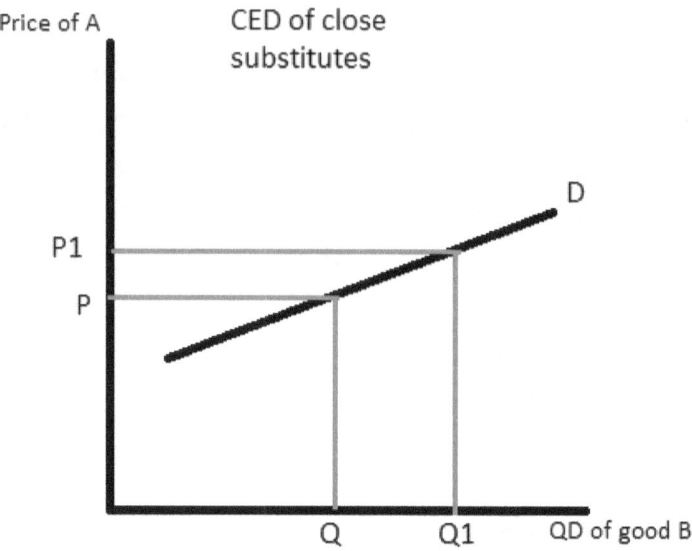

Price of A — CED of close substitutes

P1

P

Q   Q1   QD of good B

D

5. Two close complements such as gin and tonic (or gasoline and cars) would have a high negative cross elasticity of demand. If the government increases the price of the spirit by 10%, to reduce consumption and gather in more indirect tax revenue, sales of the complement tonic might fall by 25%, which is a CED of 2.5. The value is negative as the decrease in tonic sales is divided by the increase in price of gin.

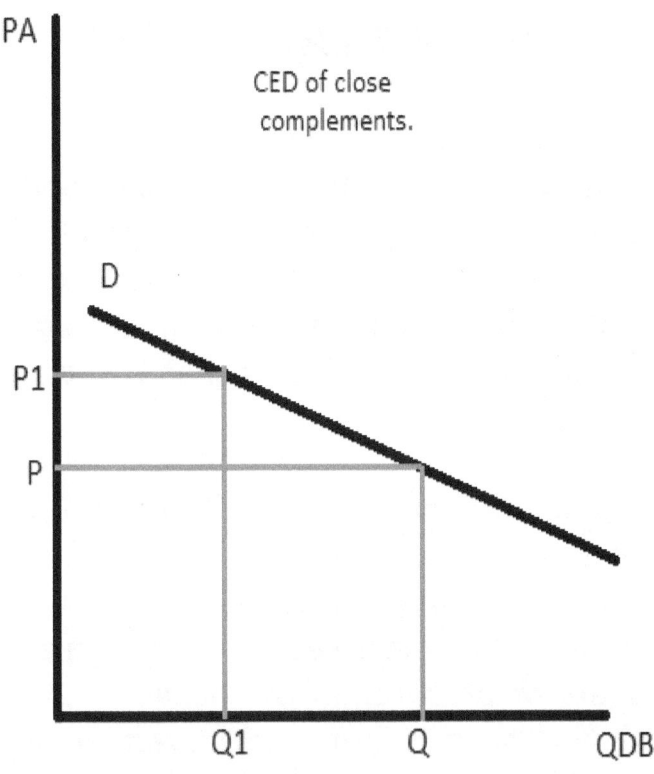

WHY DOES A SURGEON EARN MORE THAN A LABOURER?

1. Now that we have studied demand and supply, together with elasticity, it is quite easy to look at why prices are high in some markets but low in others. Looking at the labour market it is obvious that the wage earned by a surgeon is far higher than that commanded by a labourer.

2. It takes years of very demanding training to become a doctor, let alone a specialist in surgery. This creates a highly inelastic supply curve. The reason is that new surgeons cannot be magicked up out of thin air; it takes many years of preparation. A change in the level of demand, will have little or no impact on the QS of surgeons. There would be a gradual increase in surgeon numbers, if the world price rose convincingly and long term. Young doctors would decide to go into surgery rather than other areas, in response to the price signal, but this would take time to filter through the system. Additionally, the supply of surgeons is low. One way of explaining this is to think in terms of the average cost of becoming a surgeon. It is generally only the children of the well-to-do who have the financial and educational backing to enter 10 years or more of training. Supply is thus low and inelastic. In addition to inelastic supply, there is high demand for the surgeon's skills, and additionally there are no substitutes available. The

nearest substitute might be a faith healer or witch doctor! Putting inelastic low supply and inelastic high demand together creates a recipe for a high salary.

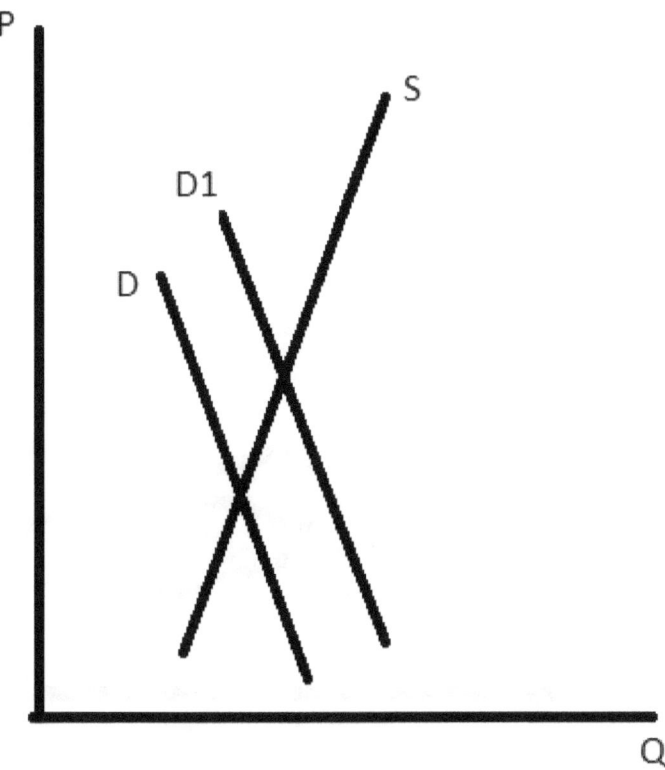

3. The unfortunate day labourer is in not such a happy position. Supply is elastic because a price rise will easily see an increase in QS. One reason is that for many jobs, little training is needed. This also explains the generally high level of supply in the industry. Demand rises and falls with the economy. In a downturn, construction workers will be the first to lose their jobs. Also, advanced machinery can now do the job of many

workers. Thus, demand is often both low and elastic. The net result of elastic high supply and elastic low demand is a low wage.

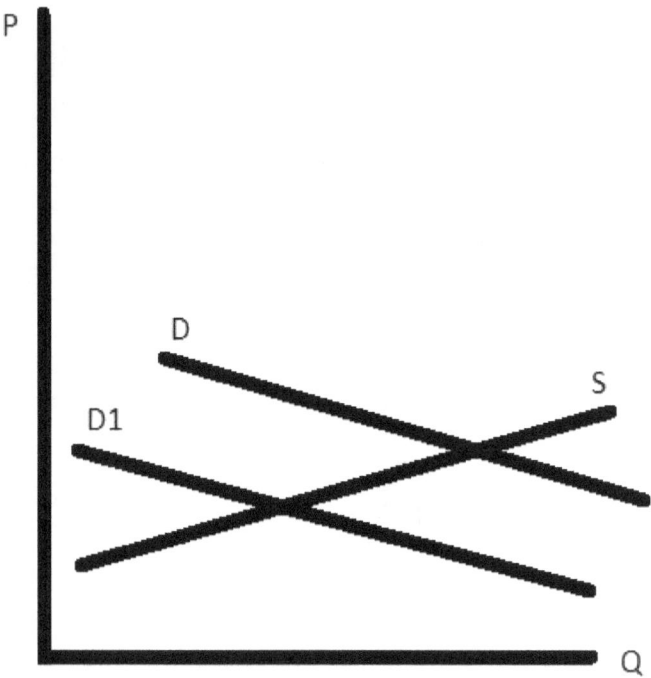

WHY DOES A PICASSO SELL FOR $180m?

1. Recent news reports of a Picasso selling for about $180m, a world record for a work of art, may get the reader thinking about why this is so. How can one picture be worth so much?

2. We have just examined elasticity. The painting in question is, of course, a unique item. This means that the supply curve it highly inelastic, one might even say perfectly inelastic.

3. We can now give some thought to demand. Demand must be very high, to inflate such a price. The reason is to be found in speculation. When share prices rise on the stock market, there is an assumption that they will keep rising, and that one should buy now while one has the chance. To do otherwise would be to miss a golden opportunity. The same applies to houses. There is an incorrect general assumption, now tempered by the property crash of 2008, that house prices only move one way. These are examples of speculative demand, and can also be seen as a case of an exceptional demand curve. This is where QD rises with the price; often this happens in the property market and the stock market. The purchaser of the unique work of art is speculating that in future the picture will be worth a lot more. It is worth noting that such speculative

purchases often end in tears. The crash in Japan in 1990 left many art investors holding Impressionist paintings worth half the purchase price.

4. The diagram which can help explain the reason a Picasso sells for such an inflated sum, would show perfectly inelastic supply and high inelastic demand. Demand is inelastic, because there are few substitutes available, as it is unusual for so called master works to appear at public auction, as most are owned by galleries.

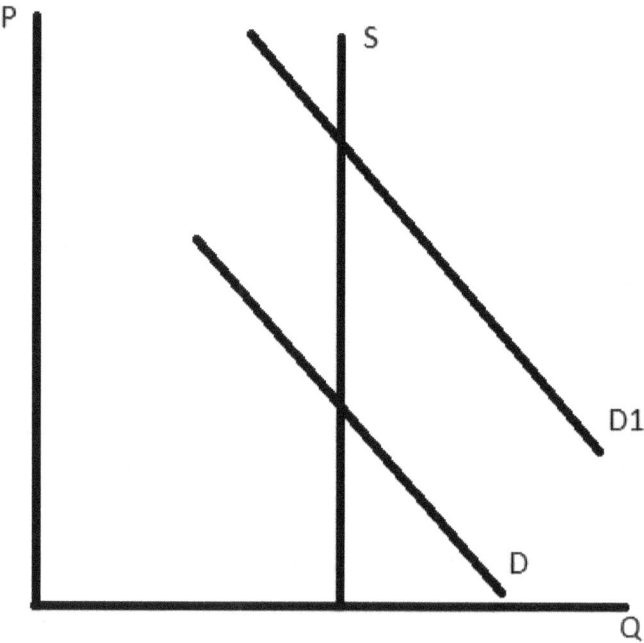

THE VOLATILITY OF PRIMARY COMMODITIES

1. Primary commodities like oil, tin, coffee, milk, lead, gold, platinum, timber, grain, tomatoes, potatoes and rice, are very price volatile. This means that they are prone to extreme and unpredictable price fluctuations (changes). Primary commodities can be seen as falling under the generic heading of all the products of farming, fishing, forestry and mining.

2. The reason for the price volatility is that primary goods are very inelastic in both demand and supply. They are inelastic in terms of price elasticity of demand because they have few substitutes, and inelastic in price elasticity of supply, because they depend on a growing season for the production, or they are very capital expensive and time consuming to extract. It is the combination of double inelasticity, which creates the recipe for extreme price volatility. Primary commodities like oil can experience a 50% change in price in a very short period of time. The best way to appreciate the reality of this situation is to firstly sketch the equilibrium diagram for a primary commodity like gold. Both demand and supply curves must have a steep gradient, indicating the inelastic nature. It should be noted, that this diagram does not, yet, show volatility. It merely sets up a picture of the starting equilibrium.

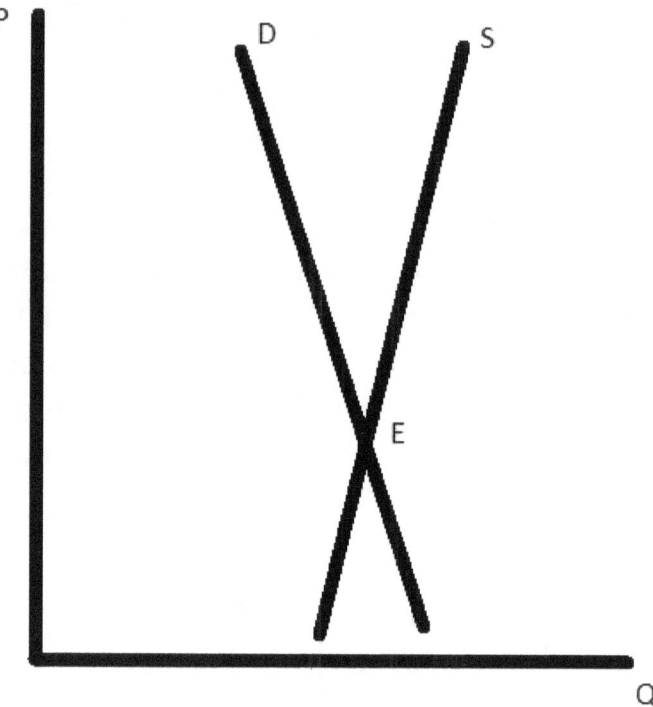

3. Now we require to superimpose an external event on the equilibrium diagram, for example an economic crisis causing the devaluation of certain currencies, for instance the euro. The devaluation of the euro might well cause an increase in demand for gold, due partly to panic buying, and partly due to speculation. The demand curve shifts to the right, in response to the perhaps modest increase in demand. As we can see from the following diagram, the effect on price is greatly intensified, due to the inelastic nature of the product. (A fall in the supply of gold, due perhaps to workers going on strike for higher wages in South

Africa, would cause the supply curve to shift to the left, causing a similar price rise).

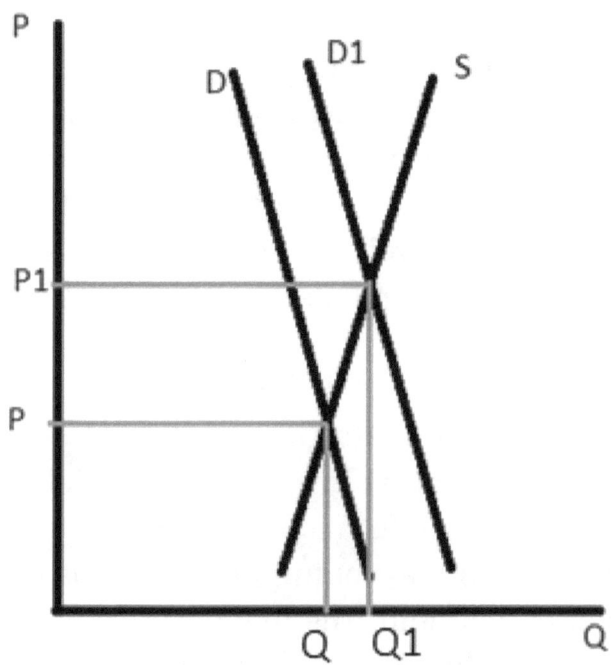

GOVERNMENT INTERVENTION

1. As agricultural primary commodities are very price volatile, governments are often tempted to intervene in the market, in order to shield and protect the low income consumer. If the price of rice is rising unreasonably, due to drought and falling supply, then many poor consumers will be unable to afford the basic necessities of life. Governments are also influenced by political expediency and the desire to gather votes at the next election, by pandering to certain groups of consumers.

2. We need to now evaluate the merits and demerits of government intervention in markets, especially markets for food and fuel. One form of intervention is where the government sets a maximum price, which is below the true market equilibrium. The market price of rice might be $2 a kilo, but the government may pass a regulation or law, specifying a price maximum of say $1. The aim may be to protect the consumer who is trying to survive on a very low income. It seems beneficial that such a law is passed, as it will ensure that the low income household can afford to eat. However, closer examination may reveal the downside of government intervention. The appropriate diagram is as follows.

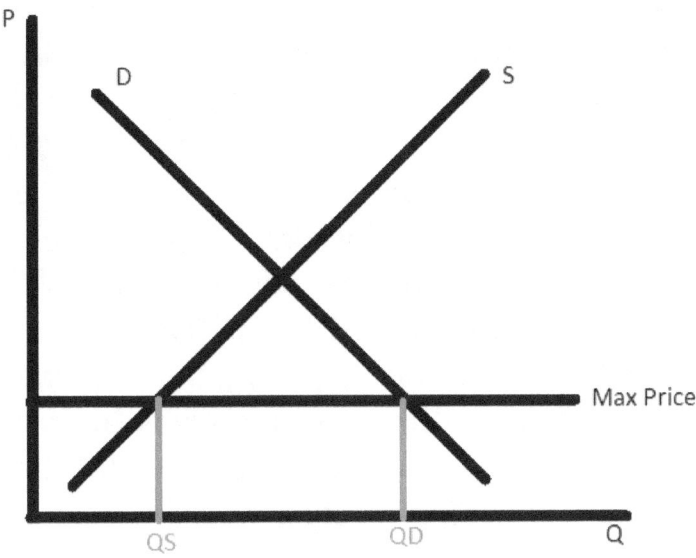

3. If we examine the diagram closely, we can see that at the artificially low price of $1, the quantity demanded far exceeds the quantity supplied, and this will lead to a severe shortage. The QD is high due to the artificially low price, while the QS is low as producers have little incentive to produce an unprofitable crop. Starvation may result, and this is ironic, considering that the aim was to prevent hardship. We can also consider that when QD exceeds QS, there will be queues and a black market. This may result in a black market price far in excess of the equilibrium true market price.

4. A maximum price below equilibrium is just one possible form of government interference in markets. Another is a minimum price above equilibrium, designed to protect the producing farmer. The aim is to ensure that the farmer has a stable income, and that he stays

farming, rather than migrating into unemployment in the city. This intervention also has some problems, because the QS will be much greater than the QD, and the surplus stock will have to be purchased by the government. The QS will be higher than QD, because the price set by law is artificially high. Often this excess produce is exported to poorer countries, fed to animals, or more likely destroyed. The EU has been guilty of these practices. The funding to pay the farmers for the surplus, must come from higher taxes, or from less spending on areas like health care and education. This is called an opportunity cost; payments to farmers mean that the same money cannot be spent on other perhaps more worthwhile causes.

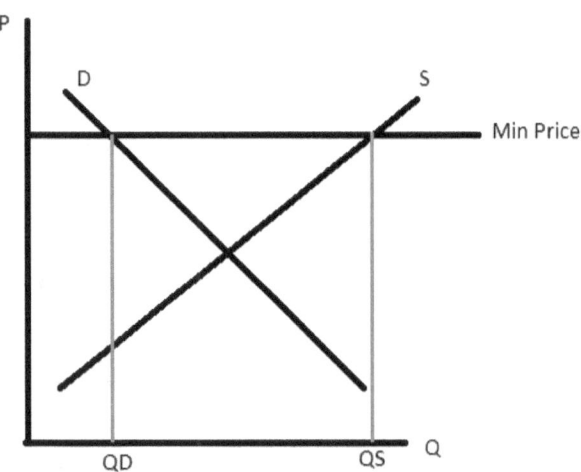

5. A buffer stock is another form of intervention. The aim is to moderate the effect of price volatility, by setting a maximum price and a minimum price, for agricultural and other products. The intention is to safeguard both

consumer and producer simultaneously. Unfortunately the buffer stock system has been less that successful in those markets, such as coffee and tin, to which it has been applied. The system requires that if there is a bumper harvest of a crop, the government will buy up the surplus and store it. They will then release the surplus, when there is a shortage sometime in the future. Unfortunately these schemes have proved very expensive in practice, and they don't work with perishable products like fruit and vegetables, unless they are frozen. Ironically the only products where buffer stock schemes have been successfully used have been in the diamond industry and to some extent the oil industry. In the diamond industry, firms like De Beers store the excess stones, and release them gradually onto the waiting market, always aiming to keep the price high.

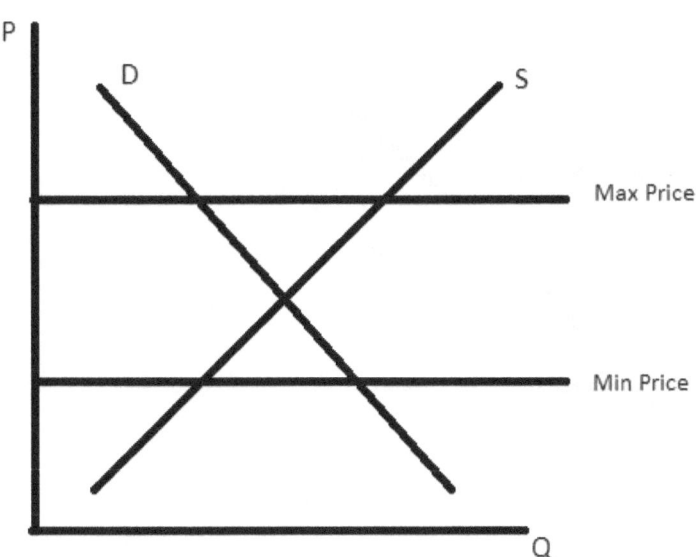

6. A subsidy is another form of intervention. The aim is to ensure a plentiful supply of food at a low price. Another aim is to reduce reliance on imports. The subsidy system to farmers in the developed world, amounts to about $1bn a day. While food availability will be encouraged, the payments to farmers have to come at the expense of high taxes and less spending on other projects. In snowbound areas of Switzerland, farming only exists due to heavy subsidies. The subsidy is shown by the supply curve shifting right, as a payment to farmers reduces their costs. The box shows the size of the subsidy, which must be paid from taxes.

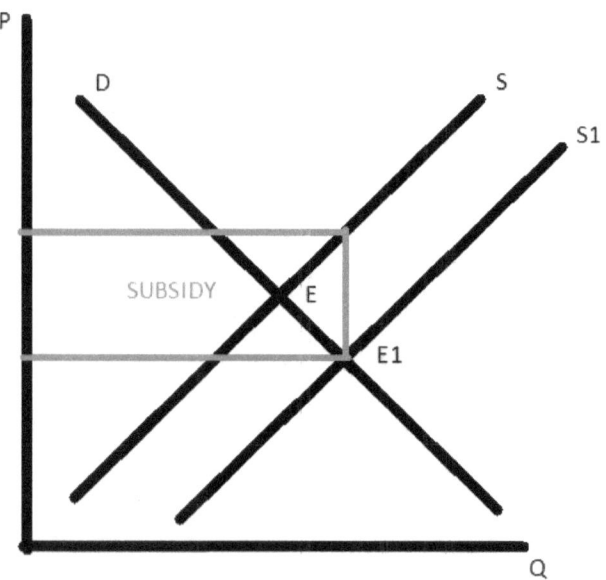

7. There are several other types of government intervention in food and other markets, for example tariffs, quotas and indirect taxes. These items will be examined in later chapters.

EXCEPTIONAL DEMAND CURVES

1. The normal demand curve is downward sloping, showing the fact that consumers respond to lower prices, by increasing quantity demanded (consumption). However there is the unusual possibility that a demand curve might be upward sloping. This is clearly exceptional, because it means that QD will rise if price rises. The exceptional demand curve is as follows.

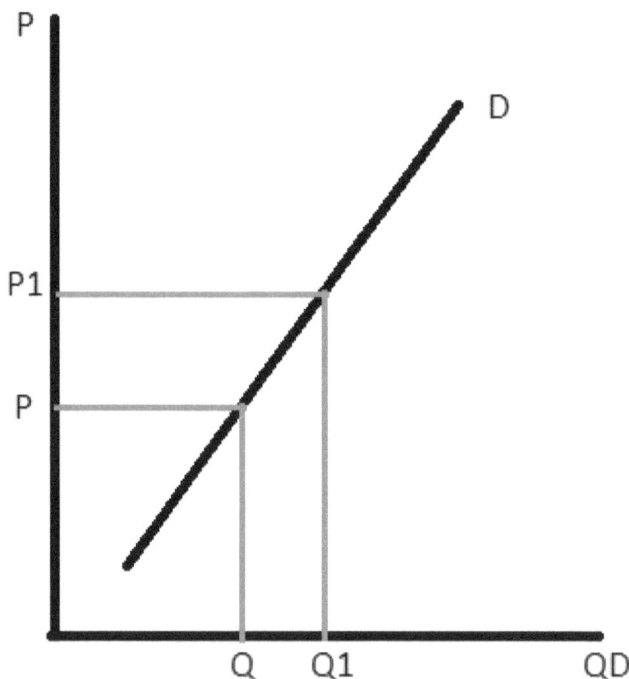

2. The situations in which an exceptional demand curve might apply are twofold. One situation relates to a special category of products called Veblen goods. A Veblen good is a product purchased at least partly for the purpose of showing off. They are also referred to as ostentatious goods. The consumer buys the good or service, at least partly as a way of displaying wealth. It is well known that certain types of good are seen as status symbols, for example a Rolex watch or a Versace dress. A Rolex is seen by the economically up-and-coming as being a way of stating that they have arrived and are successful. One rarely, if ever, sees Rolex watches on sale, as this would damage the image of the brand. With a Veblen good, a price cut would give the consumer less reason to buy the product; a 5% reduction for paying cash is one thing, but Rolex at half price would be quite another. Manufacturers of such products often prohibit retailers from selling the product as a special offer, or at a sale price, unless perhaps it is very old stock. The example of bankers celebrating a bonus with a $5000 bottle of champagne in a fancy restaurant, is another example of a Veblen good. The consumer buys a product like this perhaps solely to show he can afford it.

3. The other type of exceptional demand curve is applied to Giffen goods. These are products, usually basic foodstuffs, where a sudden steep price rise may cause QD to rise. The reason is fear of future price rises (inflation) which causes the consumer to buy more now before prices rise. This would occur where the

consumer is on a limited income and fears he may not be able to buy enough food if inflation rises and threatens to become hyperinflation.

4. It is possible to analyse the development of stock market and property bubbles, through the prism of the exceptional demand curve. Ditto the art market. As the price of shares or property or art rises, this creates an increase in QD. The reason, of course, is that as prices rise, some consumers are afraid of losing out and being left behind. They feel they will, for example, not be able to "get onto the property ladder", unless they buy a house now before prices rise further. Alternatively, one can model these events as rising speculative demand, with the demand curve shifting right. J.K. Galbraith in his book *A Short History of Financial Euphoria* (1990), discussed the development of bubbles as being a sort of financial madness, like drug induced euphoria. The classic example is Tulipomania in Holland in the 17th century, when consumers spent their entire wealth on a single tulip bulb. When sanity returned at the end of the euphoric episode, they, not surprisingly, lost all of their money.

PERFECT COMPETITION

1. There are four different market structures; perfect competition, monopolistic competition, oligopoly and monopoly. Some of these ideas may initially seem complex, but they will be explained gradually in more detail in subsequent chapters.

2. Perfect competition is a situation where there is the most intense competition imaginable. It is largely the construct of economists, and a somewhat theoretical state. There are markets in the real world which approach perfect competition, for example vibrant economies like Hong Kong, environments like the stock market, and the market for agricultural primary commodities.

3. From the standpoint of economic theory, perfect competition has certain characteristics; there is price competition, there are homogeneous (identical) products, there is perfect information and knowledge, there are no barriers to entry or exit, only normal profit is earned, there is no advertising or product differentiation, and there is efficiency in the twin senses of allocative efficiency and productive efficiency.

4. In a perfectly competitive market, competition is so intense that it drives down prices. This results in allocative efficiency, where the consumer benefits from

lowest prices and high availability. The consumer is king. There is consumer sovereignty. The formula for allocative efficiency is price=marginal cost (P=MC). Price is the same as average revenue, so an alternative formula is AR=MC. The price line, or AR curve, is another name for the demand curve. Marginal cost is the cost of making one more unit.

5. As prices are driven to the lowest point in perfect competition, firms must also strive to reduce average costs, if they are to make any profit. Thus, firms' costs are also driven down to the lowest point. This results in productive efficiency. Average costs hit the lowest point on the average cost curve. The formula is average cost=marginal cost (AC=MC). When average costs are at their lowest, this means that supply will rise, and this implies strong economic growth and prosperity.

6. The advantages of intense competition are thus shown to be consumer power, low prices, high quality, and strong economic growth with rising incomes. The producer has a harder time, as profits are low. These low profits are called "normal", meaning that the businessperson will only earn a living and be able to stay in business in the long run.

7. The purely theoretical version of perfect competition specifies that there is no difference between the products offered by firm A and firm B. There is no advertising, as this increases costs. Everyone has perfect knowledge of prices and products. It is possible

to enter and exit an industry with zero costs. It is important to appreciate the idea that competition has many benefits in the real world, and this has led economists to develop a somewhat abstracted version of reality called perfect competition. The logic behind this model is that if competition is clearly beneficial to most economic agents, then the most extreme version, called perfect competition, is worth developing and examining. Unfortunately the price of this model is a degree of abstraction and loss of realism.

8. There are, however, many markets that are approximations of perfectly competitive markets. The stock market is extremely competitive, with prices altering continuously, and one share in Microsoft is the same as another, so this is a homogeneous product. There is also extreme transparency on prices, with company information being readily available on balance sheets and profit and loss accounts. A vibrant economy like Hong Kong has little government intervention in markets, and myriad small firms competing. The market for agricultural commodities like wheat, is made up of thousands of small and medium size firms, selling an essentially similar product.

9. The diagram for perfect competition shows that the demand curve meets the lowest average cost at the profit maximising output level. There is no gap between cost and price, because the salary of the businessman is seen as a cost. The demand curve is horizontal as prices are pushed down to a uniformly low point. Firms

always try to produce at profit maximising output which is where marginal cost=marginal revenue.

10. The key idea one should take from the following perfect competition diagram, is the fact that the cost of making the product (which includes the businessman's wage), is the same as the selling price. The AC curve touches the AR curve. This means low profits. Focus only on this one point. The details of the diagram will gradually be clarified.

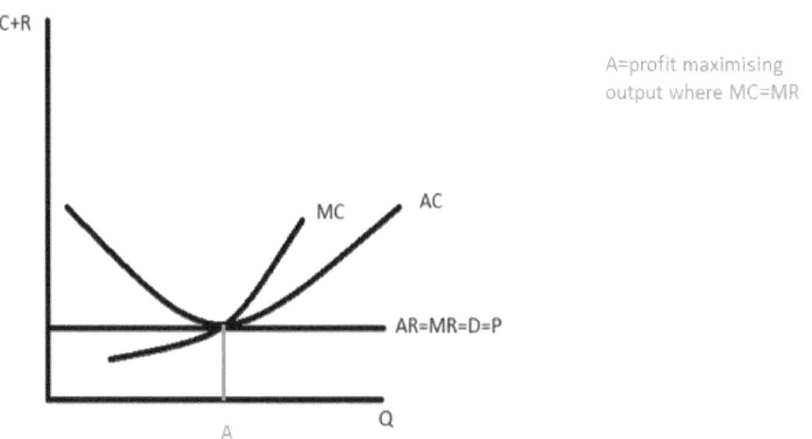

11. The most important concepts to take from the theory of perfect competition, are that competition drives prices down, while simultaneously elevating quality. Competition also drives accelerated economic growth and incomes.

MONOPOLISTIC COMPETITION

1. We have examined the market structure of perfect competition. This shows the merits of competition, against the frieze of a theoretically abstract model. The market structure of monopolistic competition is where there are a lot of small firms competing against each other. It is, if you like, the real world equivalent of perfect competition.

2. Firms in a monopolistically competitive market compete largely on price, but also to some extent through low level promotion and advertising. There is some product differentiation. Examples of this market would be bars, restaurants and hairdressers in a city. There are hundreds of small shops in a city the size of Zurich or Glasgow. Two bars might sell the same beer, but they are unlikely to charge the same price. They brand and market the product differently, depending on the precise ambience of the retail establishment. A bar designed for bikers, is marketing their product in a different way from a touristic venue.

3. Profits in this market structure are normal, meaning that you can cover all your costs in the long run, including the "cost" of your salary. Taxi drivers or barbers make a living, but they are unlikely to make a fortune, unless they move onto universalising the brand of their product. Vidal Sassoon developed a string of

branded hairdressers, and this was the development into higher profits.

4. It is possible to earn supernormal (high) profits in the short run in this market structure, if you are for example the first Sushi bar in a city, but if you make a high profit others will follow, because barriers to entry are relatively low. When we look at the following diagram, we can observe that the price line (the demand curve), is again touching the average cost curve. This illustrates normal profit, because there is no box of abnormal profit to be observed. The lack of a gap between AC and AR, tells us that only normal profits are earned. (Again, focus on this one point, rather than being concerned at this stage about other ideas being conveyed by the diagram).

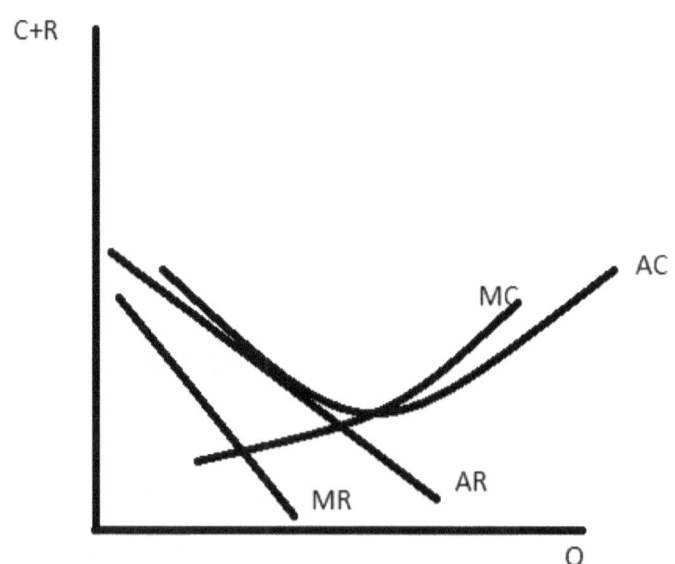

OLIGOPOLY

1. An oligopolistic market structure is when a small number of large firms control and dominate the market. Oligopoly is capital intensive with high barriers to entry. Consider the investment required to compete head to head with a firm like Samsung. Examples of industries in oligopoly would be newspapers, automobiles, pharmaceuticals, computers, luxury watches, fast food, soft drinks and branded sports gear. There may be other players in each market, but a small group dominates. This market features brands such as Toshiba and Sony, Pepsi and Coke, Samsung and Apple, Adidas and Nike.

2. An oligopolistic market can be easily represented by a pie chart with a number of key players, and a larger number of small operators.

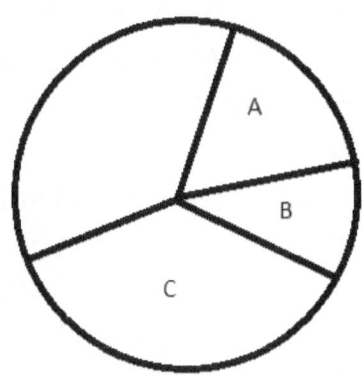

3. The characteristic feature of this market is that firms tend to avoid price competition. They operate through non-price competition, otherwise known as marketing and the 4 Ps of the marketing mix. Firms in oligopoly compete through giving careful attention to branding through product design, pricing, promotion and place of sale. For example an Apple computer will have emphasis on the product's technology and design features. The product will then be carefully priced, often using premium pricing for a newly launched product. Promotion is largely persuasive advertising, and the place of sale refers to the carefully designed Apple stores, often with their temple-like glass-staired designs. Launch days of new stores are often examples of near religious mysticism, with brands being almost the new religion.

4. Firms in oligopoly eschew price competition, because competition through lowering price is a sure way to reduce profits. Recent profits from companies like Apple and Samsung are the largest ever recorded in corporate history. This is not achieved by cost cutting to compete against rivals. Another reason for avoiding price competition is the kinked demand curve. This demand curve shows that if one firm cuts its price, other firms in the industry are very likely to follow suit, causing a price war. This means that each firm will have lower revenue and lower profits. Empirical testing suggests that this peculiar demand curve operates in oligopoly. Some firms do occasionally engage in price cutting episodes, but this usually results in large

financial losses, and in time the market reverts to its stable equilibrium of high prices and price stability. The curve below shows that if one firm price cuts from the market equilibrium, the demand curve below that point is inelastic, meaning that a price cut will increase sales, but not revenue or profits. This is due to the development of a price war; a race to the bottom as it is commonly known. Should one firm increase its price, the other firms will ignore this action, and the price increasing firm will rapidly lose market share, as shown by the elastic curve above E.

5. Firms in an oligopolistic market also tend to collude together. Collusion is where firms secretly work together to keep prices fixed high. As overt collusion is often illegal, most de facto collusion is tacit. An example of tacit collusion would be where one firm follows the barometric price leader. There is nothing illegal about charging the same price as the market leader. Occasionally examples of open overt collusion come to light, as when leading luxury hotels in Paris were illegally found to be engaging in price rigging. This sort of behaviour is designed to exploit the consumer, by creating a sort of monopoly enterprise, avoiding any real competition. Adam Smith in *The Wealth of Nations* (1776) made the point that when businessmen get together, what is often on their minds is limiting competition, to enhance profits at the expense of the consumer. Competition creates low prices and high quality.

6. Some economic commentators see a measure of real competition in oligopoly, in the form of non-collusive oligopolies. There is some recent evidence of genuine competition between players in the food supermarket industry, such as Aldi and Tesco. On the other hand, in due course, when the least efficient operators have departed into bankruptcy, the market may well revert to a more stable model to minimise losses.

7. As firms in oligopoly use tacit collusion, marketing, and the kinked demand curve, they are in a position to earn

supernormal profits in the long run. Supernormal profit just means high profits, in excess of normal profits. Supernormal profits are shown on a diagram in the form of a box of profit, created by the gap between average cost (cost of one unit) and average revenue (price of one unit). The following diagram is meant primarily to illustrate the large box of abnormal profits. This was traditionally called economic rent. The "monopoly" diagram shown below has been known to induce panic in students, so I will reiterate one last time, that the reader should focus on the one point under discussion, ignoring the apparent complexity of the diagram's immediate visual impact.

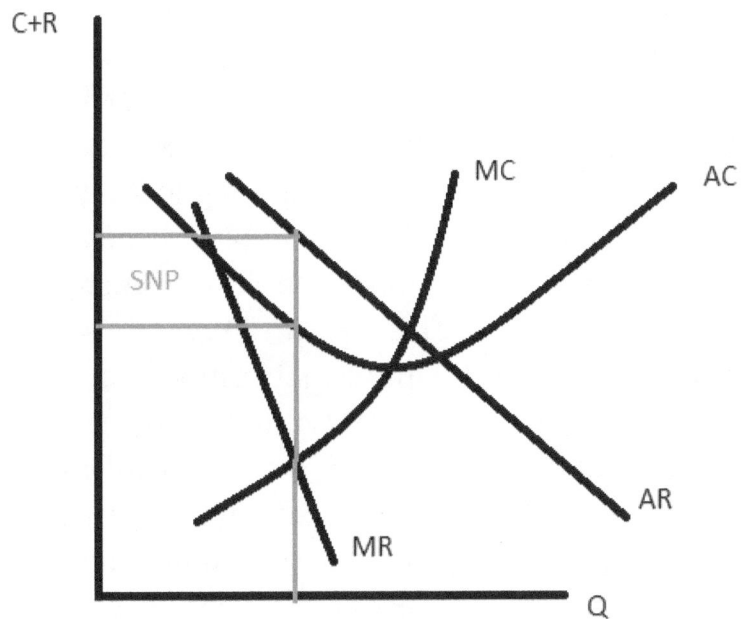

MONOPOLY

1. Monopoly is where one firm dominates in an industry. Very often there is only one rail or water or energy provider in a country. Other examples would be a firm like Microsoft, which is dominant in the provision of operating systems. Apple iTunes has effectively a monopoly grip on paid-for music and film downloads. Domination is difficult to measure legally, so many jurisdictions have set a 25% rule as being indicative of a monopoly. Often in a small town, there will be only one significant employer. Very often one firm is dominant for a period of time, and then it loses its grip on the market, and Nokia is one recent example. OPEC is the organisation of petroleum exporting countries, and it controls more than 25% of the world market for oil. De Beers is in a similar position with diamond production and exporting. Monopolists (and oligopolists) set up high barriers to entry, for example through legally protected patents or high capital investment or advertising budgets. This means that it would be extremely expensive for potential competition to enter the market. Think how hard it would be to set up a cola business in competition with the massively branded Pepsi. Pharmaceutical companies have their key drugs protected by patent, and this surrounds the product with the potential for sky-high prices and abnormal profits.

2. Monopolies are to be feared as they can control prices and exploit the consumer. They invariably earn supernormal profits at the expense of the consumer. A good example is the Microsoft Office franchise which yearly produces another version of the same system. Now it is sold as a yearly subscription, previously it was a download and before that it came as a disk. Each move is arguably towards greater consumer exploitation. The IB has a monopoly in international education, and this is reflected in the price of its online subscription Questionbanks. Previously this was sold as a one purchase disk, now it is an annual and much more expensive subscription. Students should alert themselves to the fact that as the IB is a monopoly provider, they as consumers might find themselves in a weak position, when it comes to the difficulty of some final IB exams. Mathematics HL is one such example!

3. Monopolies exploit the consumer through high prices, but also through lack of effective choice, and poor value for money. To the extent that firms in oligopoly collude, the consumer is in the same weak position. Exploitation in oligopoly tends to be through manipulation by branding and persuasive advertising. Consumers are perhaps led to believe that unless they own a Rolex watch or the latest Samsung mobile, life is not worth living!

4. At a technical level, monopoly (and to a lesser extent oligopoly) is inefficient in both the allocative and the productive sense. Firms in monopoly charge high fixed

prices which often do not deliver value for money, and this is allocatively inefficient. Output will often be limited, and this is most obvious in the oligopoly parallel; for example Patek Philippe watches. Firms in monopoly limit output to keep prices high. This is a requirement of a normal demand curve; high prices are only really possible with limited QD. As output is limited, average costs are usually high, and this means that firms are productively inefficient, keeping supply and economic growth slow. This means that monopoly firms are inefficient in that consumer sovereignty is damaged, and inefficient as economic growth is not propelled by competition.

5. There are some commentators who feel that the critique of monopoly (and by extension oligopoly) is unfounded. The most celebrated is Joseph Schumpeter, who in his famous book *Capitalism, Socialism and Democracy* (1942), argued that perfect competition is a fiction which in any case leads to profits which are too low to finance reinvestment. He convincingly argues that we should not fear monopoly, as the gale of creative destruction will soon destroy the present monopolists, as they grow lazy and complacent on the back of growing profits. The fate of Sony computers and Nokia phones and Blackberry, tends to lend some support to Schumpeter's position. Following on with Schumpeter's theme that monopolies may be beneficial, it is indeed clear that monopoly has some obvious advantages in that there are high profits available for reinvestment and this can lead to

innovative products. Research and development is extremely expensive and Microsoft and Apple plough back a lot of their abnormal profits into this zone. These large businesses also provide jobs and export potential, for example the large Japanese exporting oligopolies. When Japan's domestic economy was in tatters after the 1990 stock market crash, exports saved the day. Another possible plus with large imperfectly competitive firms is that they have economies of scale. This is the idea that their large size allows for a reduction in average costs. This point can be illustrated on the following diagram.

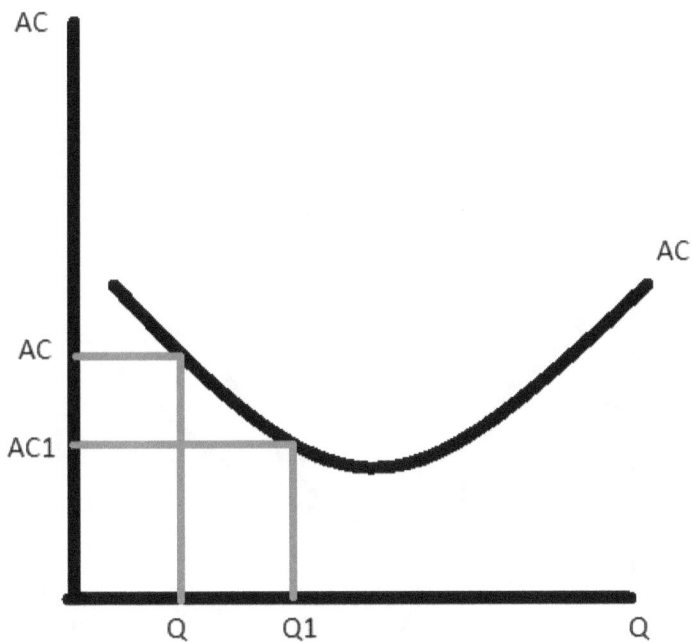

6. The diagram of abnormal profits used previously for collusive oligopoly is also appropriate for monopoly. At this point, however, we can focus on the fact that all firms in the long run, in a capitalist system, try to maximise profits at the point where marginal costs are equal to marginal revenue (MC=MR). This is the profit maximising formula. What it means is that firms will endeavour to find the quantity of a product to produce, which will maximise their profits. Marginal cost is the cost of making one extra unit, while marginal revenue is the revenue gained from selling one extra unit. We can see from the following diagram that at profit maximising output, the price in monopoly is very high, and average costs are not at the bottom of the curve.

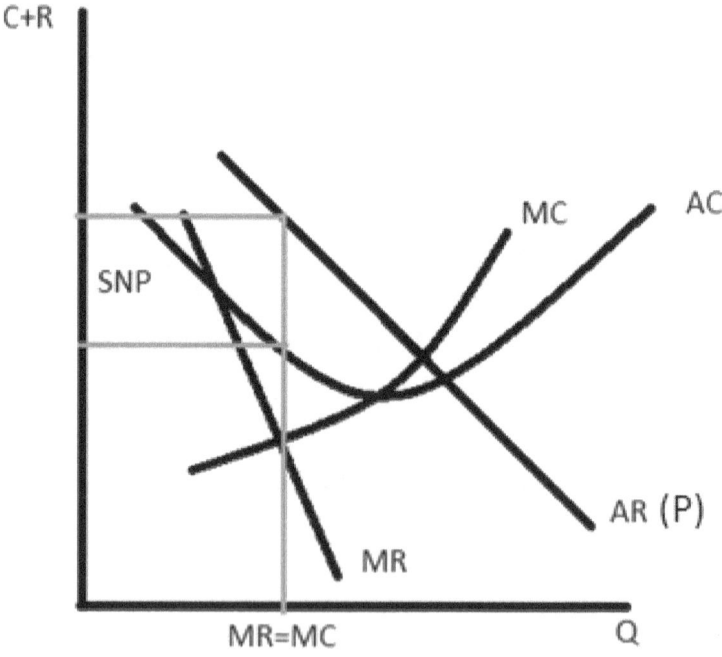

7. Price discrimination is relevant in the context of monopoly power. Price discrimination arises when a firm charges different prices to different groups of consumers, for what is basically the same product. This is only possible if the firm has a degree of monopoly power, and the elasticity of demand is different in each consumer market. An example would be where the service of a journey from Cambridge to London by train is much more expensive during the rush hour. The reason is that some consumers must travel to work at that time, there is thus an inelastic market, and the price can be increased. There is also a certain monopoly power, because travel into London is not very practical by car during the rush hour, so train has a monopoly.

8. Monopoly has a further application in the concept of a contestable market. This is where there is a monopoly, but other firms could enter the market if they wanted to. There may be one monopoly provider of coach travel between two remote Scottish locations, however there are low barriers to entry, meaning that another firm could enter into competition fairly cheaply, if they wanted to do so. A contestable market is a monopoly situation where profits will be normal. If the firm puts up its price beyond an acceptable level, competition will soon enter the market.

MARKET FAILURE

1. The free market capitalist system has brought untold wealth to millions of people, through the important role given to competition. Perfect competition creates low prices, high quality, consumer sovereignty, power and choice. Productive efficiency through competition delivers economic growth with rising income levels, growing year on year in a compound way, so that incomes can easily double in a few short years in a fast growing economy like China. However, capitalism is not without its flaws and blemishes, and this is what is commonly known as market failure.

2. The free market is considered to fail in a range of important ways. There is massive income and wealth inequality, with a pyramid structure of a few wealthy folk, and millions of poor worker ants at the bottom of the pile.

3. Another failure is the fact that profit maximisation at the point MR=MC, means that often the environment is damaged through pollution and destruction of irreplaceable resources. Firms in a capitalist system don't consider the effect of their profit making activities on the broader social environment. They produce at marginal cost=marginal revenue, not the point where marginal social cost=marginal social benefit. This leads to a welfare loss, in the form of excessive pollution.

What does it benefit a man if he has a few extra dollars in his pocket, but can't breathe the air surrounding him?

4. The capitalist system tends to focus on short term profit, because this reduces risk. Often the long term implications are ignored. The lead up to the 2008 crisis is an example of short-termism, where investment banks and mortgage brokers were deliberately or negligently ignoring the effect of their securitised bond sales in the long term. So long as the music continued to play, they all continued to dance to the tune of high finance.

5. Another critique of capitalism is the fact that products like alcohol, tobacco, pornography, drugs and fast food are very freely available. This is the outcome of a free society; freedom means freedom to demand the products you desire, and a firm will duly supply them. These products, which are more freely available the freer the society, are known as demerit goods, as they are damaging to the consumer and society as a whole. There is over-production and over-consumption of demerit goods in a capitalist society. Demerit goods have social costs. The formula for social cost is private cost + negative externality. This means that over-consumption of tobacco will damage the consumer, but it will also have the negative externality of damaging society as a whole, through working days lost and increased spending on health care. A diagram of negative externalities is as follows.

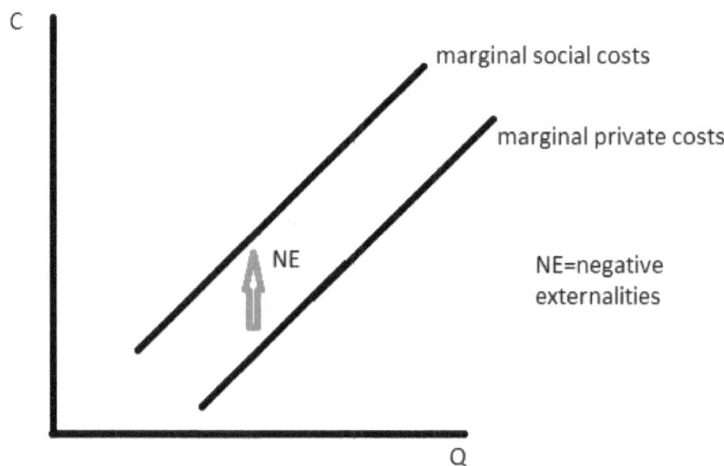

6. The free society delivered on the capitalist model also under-provides and under-consumes merit goods. Merit goods are goods which have a social benefit, which is defined as being private benefit+positive externality. A positive externality is a positive effect on society as a whole. For example a consumer of education will hopefully be able to improve not just his own life, but his society in the long term. Examples of merit goods would be health care and education. These are produced by the free market, but they tend to be very expensive, and thus only fully available to the financial elite. Positive externalities can also be diagrammatically illustrated.

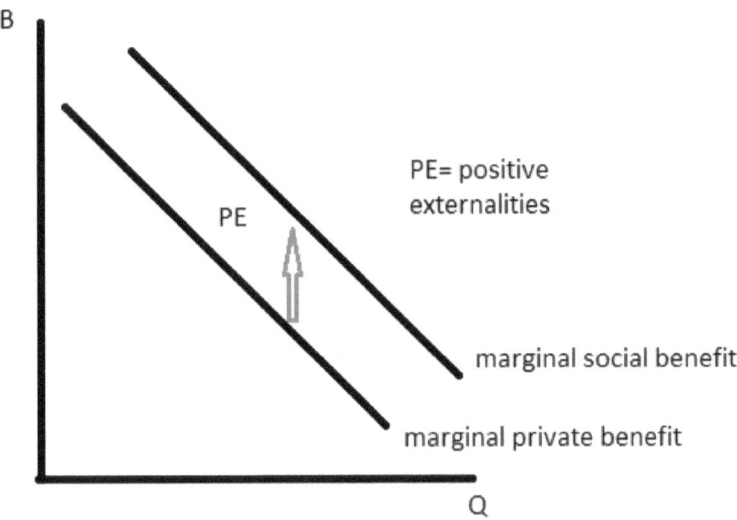

B

PE

PE= positive
externalities

marginal social benefit

marginal private benefit

Q

7. Another weakness or flaw with the model of capitalism is the fact that the free market is very good at producing most types of product, for example food, clothing, watches, houses, or even education. However there are certain types of product, known as public goods, which the free market cannot readily produce. The reason is that these products cannot be easily directly charged for by the business. Yet, these goods or services are essential to human life. Examples would be police, fire-service, lighthouses, army, roads, street lighting and the legal system. These products have certain philosophical characteristics which make them unsuitable for production by private firms. They are non-rival, meaning that one person's consumption does not reduce another person's consumption. If I enjoy street lighting, this does not stop another passer-by enjoying the same benefit. Private goods are rival; if I

eat part of a cake there is less left for someone else. Public goods are also non-excludable. If someone is assaulted in the street, the police cannot refuse to investigate the crime, just because the victim cannot pay. You cannot let one person consume the product, while excluding another. This is very different from a good like education, where a school can refuse to let a student enter the classroom if he has not paid his fees. The capitalist system is competent at producing almost all goods and services, but it cannot easily produce public goods, defined as those goods which are non-rival and non-excludable. The main reason is that private firms are unable to charge the consumer directly for the good or service provided. This effectively means that the state has to provide these goods through the medium of taxation.

8. Another weakness of the capitalist free market is that it inevitably generates oligopolies and monopolies which exploit the consumer, and reduce economic growth. These are examples of imperfect competition. If we consider Russia after the decay of communism; within a few short months the oligarchs had taken control of key aspects of the economy. This backfired on them when Putin interceded to repossess some of the nation's pilfered assets.

9. A final failure of the free market is the immobility of certain factors of production, coupled with imperfect knowledge. It is not easy for workers to relocate to a part of the country where there are opportunities. In a

free market everything costs money, and rent in areas of low unemployment is usually high. An example would be the Mecca of London where there are many jobs, but unemployed workers in the north of England and Scotland often cannot afford to relocate.

SOLUTIONS TO MARKET FAILURE

1. The problems of market failure have some solutions. It is important to appreciate that one main economic justification for the existence of government is that government can address the problems of market failure and try to solve these issues.

2. Government can solve the problem of the absence of public goods, by providing these goods through the medium of taxation. Thus, police, fire brigade, army and legal system can be financed through taxation. Public goods like roads can also be created in a similar way, but some roads can be provided by the private sector. An example of a privately provided road would be a toll road. As technology advances more roads can be offered by the private sector; firms can build and maintain them, and charge directly for their use.

3. Merit goods like health care and education are provided by the free market system, but extra merit goods can be provided through taxation, to ensure that all citizens have provision of basic health care and education. Adam Smith argued that the inequality created by capitalism could be partly addressed through universal primary education being offered through taxes by government.

4. The problem of pollution can be addressed through stricter laws and regulations limiting the type and amount of pollutants. Another approach is to use indirect taxes to encourage a reduction in pollution. If firms pollute above a certain strict limit, they will pay in taxes. A further strategy is a system of pollution permits, where firms can sell their right to pollute to other companies. This encourages all firms to reduce pollution to enhance their profits. One dilemma with pollution is that economic growth creates pollution, and the faster the growth the more pollution is likely to ensue. The unregulated growth of certain Asian countries is an example of this problem. Through a combination of carrots and sticks, pollution can be controlled, and this is shown on the following diagram. Output level A is where there is excessive unregulated economic growth and excess pollution. China is an example of an economy suffering from this problem. Marginal social costs exceed marginal social benefits at this fast unregulated rate of economic growth. This means that the overall benefits of the unregulated growth are exceeded by the overall disadvantages. Having a slightly higher income, and access to more material goods, hardly compensates for not being able to breathe clean air. High levels of pollution pose a deadly health risk, and life expectancy can plummet. The area marked welfare loss, shows the overall loss to society of the excessive pollution. It is important to appreciate that pollution is inevitable, but a balance must be struck with nature. Economic activity causes

pollution, and zero pollution implies that human life would vanish.

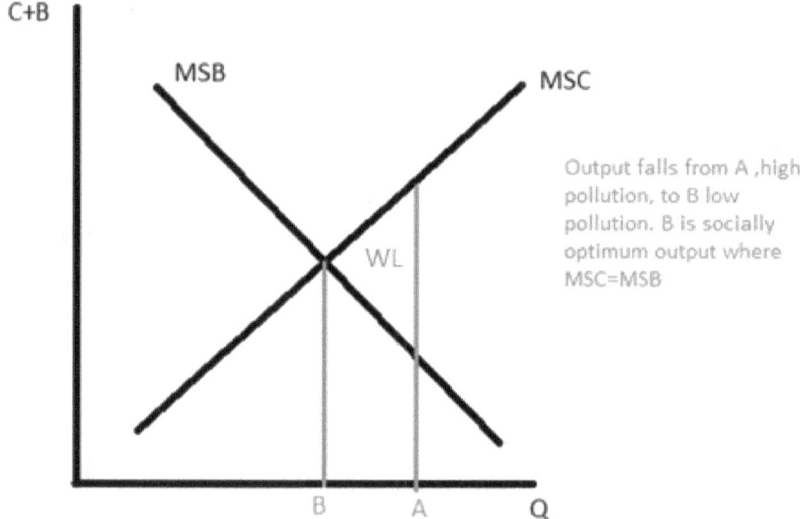

5. The inequality of income and wealth distribution can be addressed through a system of progressive taxation, where high income earners pay a higher percentage of their income in taxation. The tax revenue can then be used to fund welfare payments, health provision and improved education for all. A progressive tax system is where a worker earning £20,000 might pay 10% tax, while a worker earning £30,000 might pay 10% on the first £20,000 earned, but 15% on the next £10,000. High earners might pay 50% tax on incomes above £100,000. One argument against this system is that it can discourage enterprise, and thus economic growth might suffer. The argument against progressive tax is that it removes incentives to work hard and take risks.

At certain times the highest tax band in the UK was 90%. This encourages tax evasion and a brain drain, where highly skilled workers leave the country. Arguments in favour of proportional taxation are gathering strength in some circles. This is a system of taxation where everyone pays the same rate of taxation, irrespective of income level. For example a worker earning £20,000 and a worker earning £200,000 would each pay a flat rate of say 20% in tax. This means that the wealthy worker is still paying much more tax in money terms, even if the % stays the same.

6. The problem of overconsumption of demerit goods like tobacco and alcohol can be attacked through a combination of negative state-funded publicity, and indirect taxation. The government can fund adverts designed to persuade consumers to reduce or stop consumption of demerit goods. This involves stealing the tricks of the big oligopolistic firms, to persuade citizens to amend their behaviour. Negative persuasive adverts against smoking have been successfully implemented in the UK and other countries. It is now seen by young people in the UK as being rather "uncool" to smoke. This is in contrast to some other countries like Switzerland, where there is no such social stigma. Indirect taxation involves putting high taxes on demerit goods, with a view to reducing consumption. One problem is that the addictive nature of these products makes it very hard for consumers to stop using the good, in spite of high prices. Often the citizen will continue to drink and smoke, even if his children

risk going hungry. The diagram showing indirect taxes on alcohol illustrates that the fall in consumption may not be great, due to the fact that demerit goods are inelastic in terms of demand.

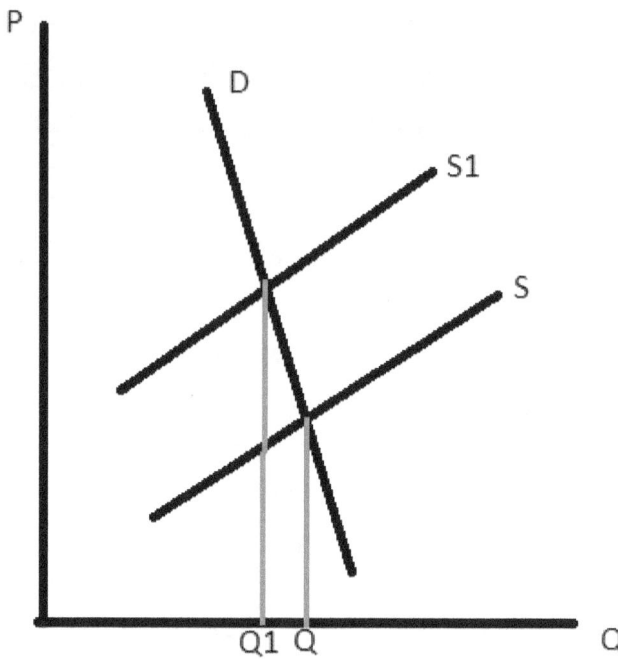

7. It is well known that firms in imperfect competition, that is to say monopolists and oligopolists, are responsible for the exploitation of the consumer. This is a major form of market failure. These firms charge high prices for products which might not represent value for money. One blatant form of exploitation is the brain washing and manipulation of the consumer by persuasive advertising. The whole marketing process

can be criticised as being a form of consumer exploitation. Consumers are sold a dream that their life will only be improved if they purchase a particular brand of product, be it a pair of Nike trainers, a Breitling watch or an Apple computer. Government can regulate to break up or fine monopolies if their conduct is deemed prejudicial to the consumer, however, often the monopolist can afford the best legal representation and can pour vast sums into fighting against the often underfunded government agency. The monopolist or oligopolist can hire a lawyer with a strong financial incentive to succeed, while the government lawyer may often be underpaid, perhaps underskilled, and overworked.

8. Problems of short-termism have solutions. It is possible to hold back bonuses paid to bankers for a period of say 5 years, to ensure that their profit generating activities serve the long term economic good, rather than just short term greed and expediency.

9. Lack of information about job vacancies and lack of mobility by workers can be dealt with through a government subsidy. The government can for instance subsidise relocation, and provide good databanks of job availability.

10.If would be most naïve to believe that the forms of market failure can be easily or fully solved. The government can employ tactics that will reduce the failings of the market, but these problems will never fully vanish. The capitalist, free market system, is far from perfect and some of the failings are alarming, but it is one of the best human systems of economic organisation so far devised. The economist J K Galbraith in his book *The Affluent Society* (revised edition 1984), wrote extensively about the failings of the market. He saw capitalism as driven to produce more and more material goods, and in North America, and other countries, he observed the development of extreme crass materialism. Consumers had the latest huge TV screen or computer console or gas guzzling motor vehicle, but there was gross underspending on merit goods, and under provision of public goods. He advised government to tax materialism more severely, using the proceeds to fund the extension, through tax revenue, of merit and public goods such as better schools and universal health care, public parks and recreation facilities, libraries and walkways, rather than the bill-boarded world of branded commercialism.

WHO PAYS THE TAX?

1. When an indirect tax is placed on a product such as cigarettes, this can be used by the state to encourage a reduction in consumption of a demerit good. Demerit goods have high social costs. The formula for a social cost is; social cost=private cost + negative externality. Another reason for the imposition of the tax, is to achieve high tax revenue. As demerit goods are highly inelastic, consumption will not fall by a huge amount, and the tax revenue can be used to finance government spending or to reduce other forms of taxation, such as income tax, known as direct tax. Income tax is called direct tax, because in most countries, the income earner has the tax deducted at source from his pay, at the end of each month, on a pay-as-you-earn basis. Tax on items like alcohol or tobacco or gasoline are called indirect, because you only have to pay the tax if you choose to buy the product. The ethics of placing high taxes on gasoline and cigarettes has often been debated. Many poorer consumers need to drive to get to work, so they are being penalised. Similarly, addictive behaviours like smoking or heavy alcohol consumption are more likely to be indulged in by the socially and economically unfortunate.

2. When a high indirect tax is imposed, this is shown by the supply curve shifting to the left, because the firm has to pay the tax to the government on each pack of

cigarettes sold. However, the firm will try hard to pass on the taxation in the form of higher prices, so that the firm's profits don't decrease by any more than is necessary. The business will usually be successful in this strategy, so long as the products are inelastic in demand. Products like gasoline, tobacco and alcohol are inelastic due to being either essential or addictive. The basic rule is that so long as the price elasticity of demand is more inelastic than the price elasticity of supply, the consumer will carry most of the tax burden. Another way of saying this is that if demand is more inelastic than supply, the consumer pays more of the tax. The diagram below shows the box of tax revenue, and most of this is effectively paid by the consumer in the form of a price rise.

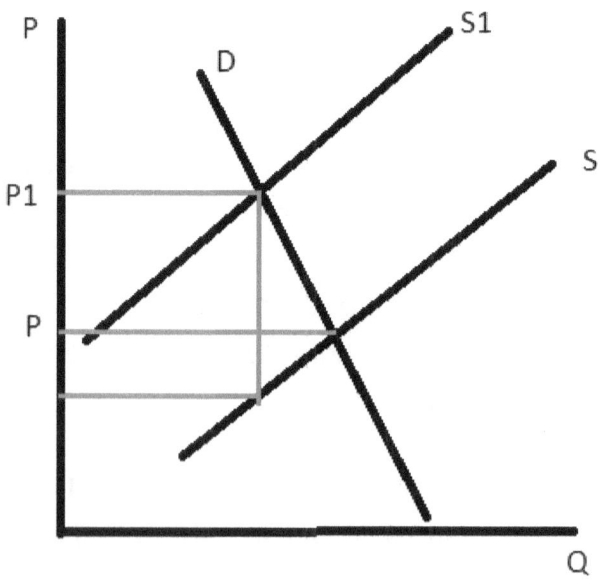

3. The government targets demerit goods for heavy indirect tax, because consumption will not vanish due to high taxes. If the government were to impose high indirect taxes on elastic products like tourism, then consumption would sharply decline, and jobs would be instantly lost.

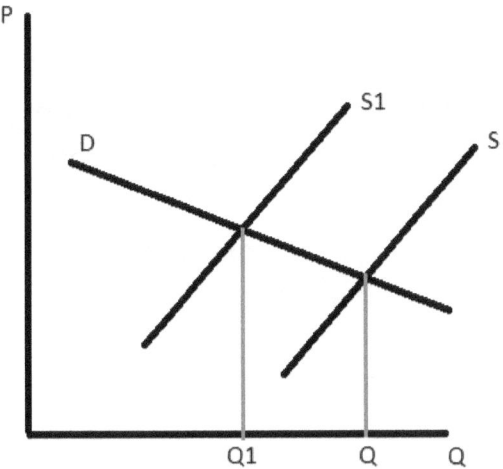

job losses shown by Q to Q1

OUTPUT DECISIONS

1. Firms in a free market aim in the long run to maximise profits. This is the main aim of most firms operating in the capitalist system. The formula for profit maximisation is marginal cost=marginal revenue (MC=MR), however the logic of this equation requires to be explained. Marginal cost is the cost of making one extra unit, and marginal revenue is the income derived from selling one more unit. Diagrammatically the marginal revenue curve and the marginal cost curve look as follows. This is a de facto representation of the cost and revenue profile of an average firm.

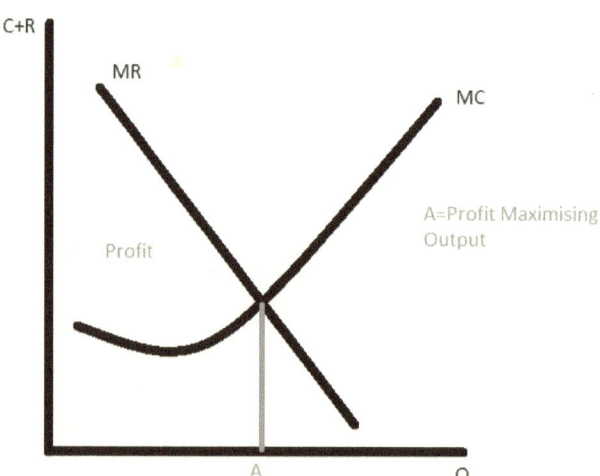

2. If we look between these two curves, we can see that as output is increased from zero, there is a gap between MR and MC. This gap is a strip of profit, which

may represent the profit from making and selling one more unit. The business will continue to increase output until the gap vanishes. The reason is that every strip represents a strip of profit, and total profit is the addition or sum of all the strips. At the point where MC=MR, there is an incentive to stop increasing output, because continuing to increase output would reduce overall profit, as beyond the MC=MR point, the MC line is above the MR line.

3. Firms in a capitalist system will aim in the long run to maximise profits. The long run is defined in economics as how long it takes to change all factors of production; land, labour, capital and entrepreneurship. The long run also corresponds more generally to a long period of time.

4. The short run corresponds to a shorter time span, and is formally defined as being the time during which at least one factor is fixed. For example it may take a certain period of time to replace a skilled worker, or for a worker's contract to expire.

5. In the short run, firms may have different aims. They may want to maximise revenue rather than profit. The reason is that maximising revenue may well correspond to increasing market share. The firm can then put the price up, when market share has been gained, and some competitors have been eliminated. The aim of revenue maximisation is also popular with sales departments, as their pay may be based on

commission. The formula for revenue maximisation is marginal revenue=zero (MR=0). This represents the idea that selling one more unit after MR=0, would cause total revenue to decline, as the marginal revenue would be negative.

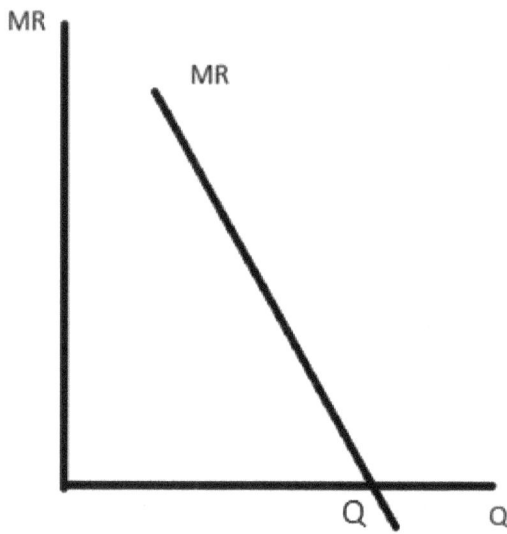

6. It is important to point out that each output aim, creates a quantity of output. The quantity a firm produces if it aims to maximise profit, will be less than the quantity it produces if it wants to maximise revenue. The normal demand curve shows that the lower the output the higher the price. This indicates that in a capitalist environment prices are held high by imperfect competition in the form of oligopolies and monopolies. Profit maximising output often corresponds to a high price.

7. A firm may engage in so called predatory pricing, where they deliberately select a low price with the aim of destroying the competition. Needless to say, when the market is clear of the competition, the firm will increase the price, as they will have more market power, perhaps as a monopolist.

8. A firm operating under some measure of government control may be instructed to produce at the level of productive efficiency, meaning lowest average cost. This would be an output level designed to minimise average cost. This might allow scarce resources to be preserved for a longer time span. The output quantity would be at the point MC=AC, which is the lowest point on the AC curve.

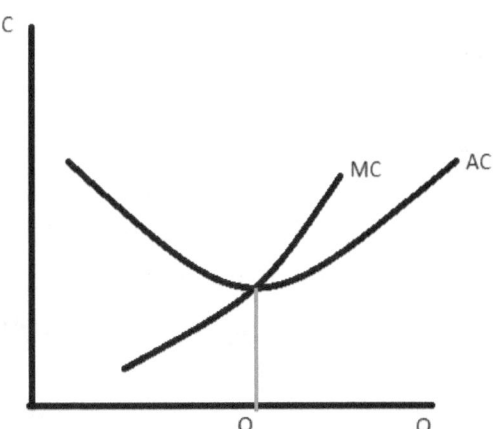

9. Another possibility is that a socialist government might decree that certain firms produce at the level of allocative efficiency. This is where output levels are

higher than profit maximising output, and prices are much lower. The formula is P=MC or AR=MC.

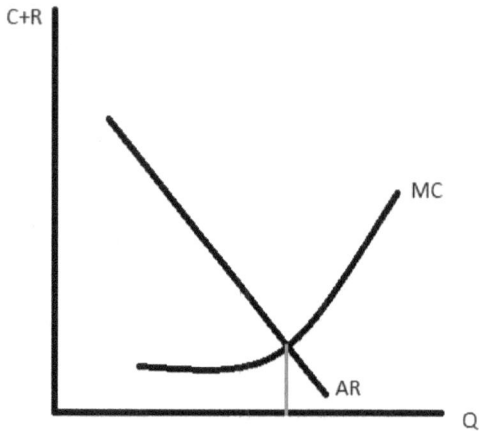

10. We can construct a diagram showing the output levels corresponding to profit maximisation, revenue maximisation, productive efficiency and allocative efficiency. It will be observed that as one moves through this list, output rises and price falls. What is most remarkable is that the capitalist model produces at profit maximising output, where price is relatively high and output is relatively low. Often in a free market, products will be only available at a high price and with limited availability. An extreme example would be an exclusive Swiss watch such as Patek, where only a few timepieces are available in a retail outlet, at very high unit price. To charge a high price you must be exclusive and limit output; the demand curve requires this.

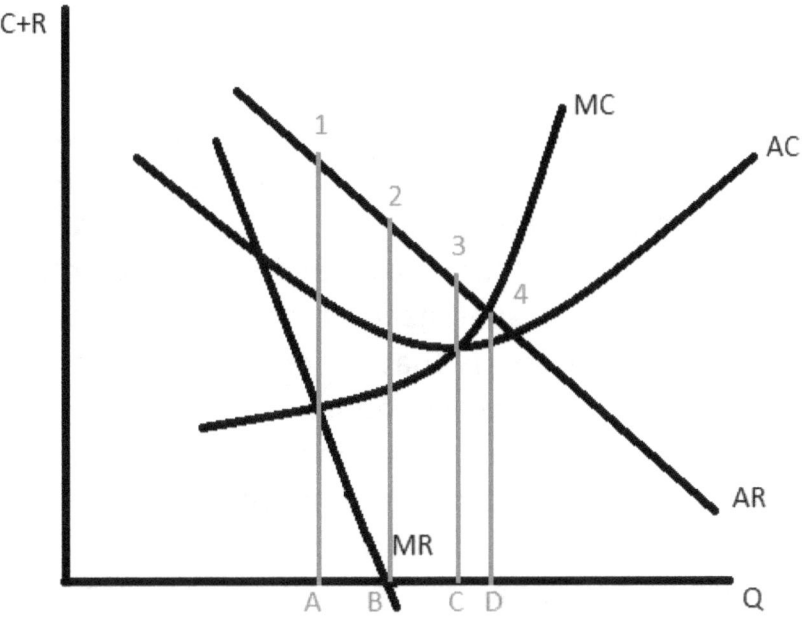

11. A is profit maximising output at MC=MR. B is revenue maximisation at MR=0. C is productive efficiency at AC=MC. D is allocative efficiency at AR=MC. As we move from A to D, prices are seen to fall from their highest in capitalist profit maximisation, to the lowest in allocative efficiency. In a capitalist system, allocative efficiency and productive efficiency are only achieved in perfect competition. The more intense the competition, the closer A, B, C and D are to each other. In the monopolist/oligopolist diagram above, these output and price points are far apart. This is indicative of the lack of efficiency and exploitative nature of imperfect competition.

COSTS

1. Firms have to deal with a number of different types of cost. Average cost is the cost of making one unit, for example one computer or a pair of shoes. It is calculated by taking total costs and dividing by output. The shape of the average cost curve is similar to a parabola. The reason is that average costs start to fall as output rises, due to economies of scale. For example a larger firm can buy raw materials in bulk at a discount, and they can make more efficient use of machinery, running it to nearer capacity. A big firm can also employ specialists in areas like marketing, production and finance, who will increase the firm's productivity. Productivity is the amount a worker produces in a period of time, traditionally one hour. As a firm gets too big, it becomes unwieldy and encounters diseconomies of scale. This causes average costs to rise. The main diseconomies are managerial, where communication and motivation break down. An extreme example of diseconomies of scale would be the Soviet Union, where bureaucrats attempted to direct the whole economy. This system proved very inefficient in comparison to more competitive economies like the US. Ultimately the Soviet Union failed from an economic point of view due to managerial diseconomies of scale.

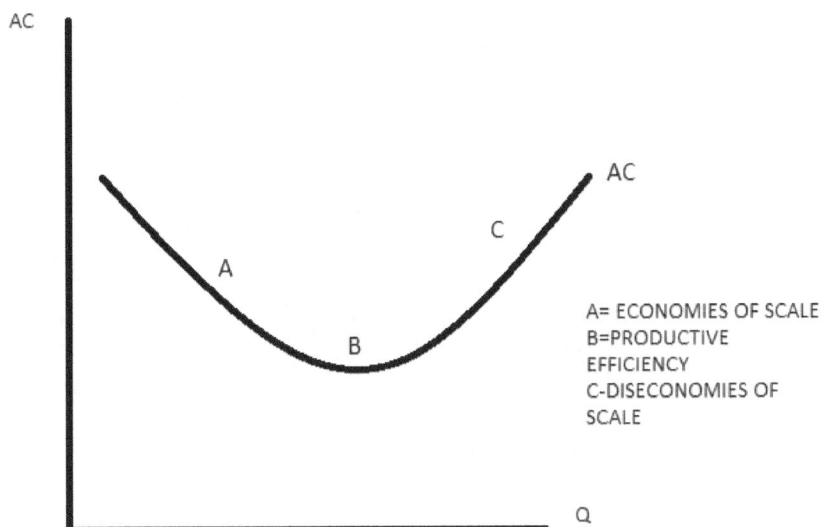

AC

AC

C

A

B

A= ECONOMIES OF SCALE
B=PRODUCTIVE
EFFICIENCY
C-DISECONOMIES OF
SCALE

Q

2. Total costs are composed of fixed costs and variable costs. Fixed costs are items like rent or a manager's salary, which stay fixed and do not depend on the level of output. You have to pay the factory rent, whether you produce 10 units or 100 a day. Variable costs alter depending on the level of output. It should be clear that making 100 pairs of shoes requires more leather, energy and labour than 10 pairs. Clearly some costs don't fit neatly under the heading of fixed or variable; if output continues to grow, the factory will have to expand its premises and pay extra rent. Thus the terms semi-fixed or semi-variable are sometimes used.

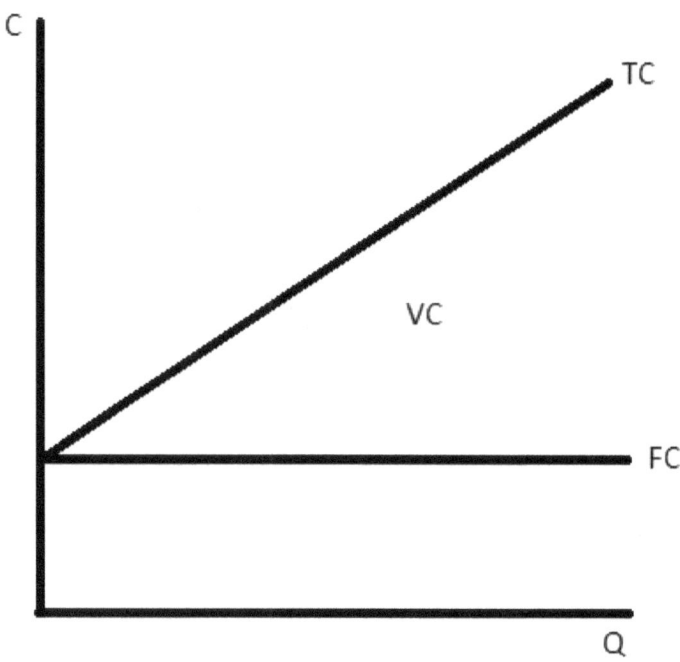

3. Marginal cost is the cost of making one extra unit. Marginal cost (and revenue) were introduced primarily by Alfred Marshall towards the end of the 19th century, and proved a breakthrough in economic analysis. The relationship between average costs and marginal costs is shown in the next diagram. Average costs start higher than marginal costs, because average costs include a fixed and a variable component, while marginal costs are only variable. However, when diseconomies of scale enter the picture, the cost of making the next unit exceeds the average cost, because the average cost is kept down by the average fixed cost getting smaller as output rises.

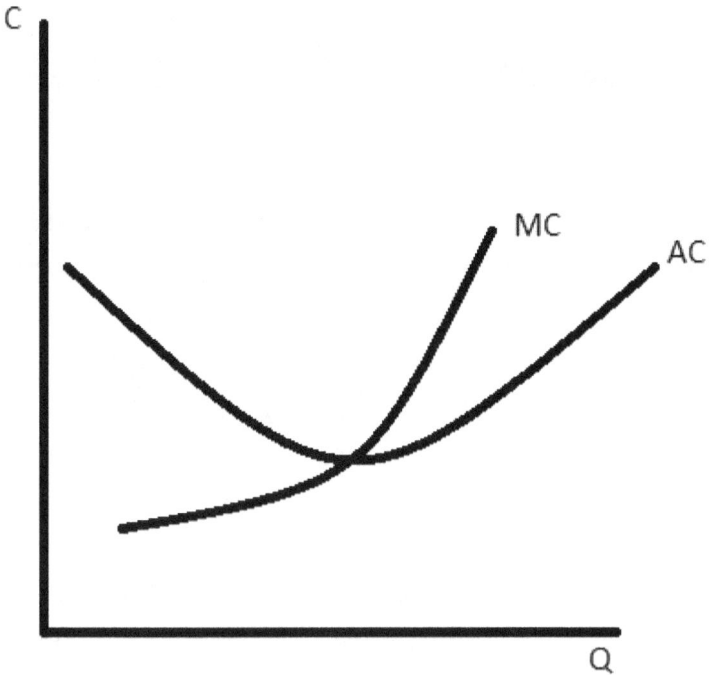

DECREASING RETURNS TO SCALE AND DIMINISHING MARGINAL RETURNS

1. When a firm increases in size, it can begin to enjoy economies of scale. One example would be raw materials bought in bulk at a discount. This causes average costs to fall. However in the long run, the firm may change all of its factors of production and eventually grow too large to be manageable. At this point, due to managerial diseconomies of scale, average costs start to rise. This is what is known as decreasing returns to scale. Decreasing returns to scale is a long run phenomenon, which focuses on the idea of a firm changing all its factors of production, perhaps on a continuous basis, until it becomes too large to function efficiently. It becomes productively very inefficient. A school with 5000 students would suffer from communication and motivation issues due to its unwieldy size.

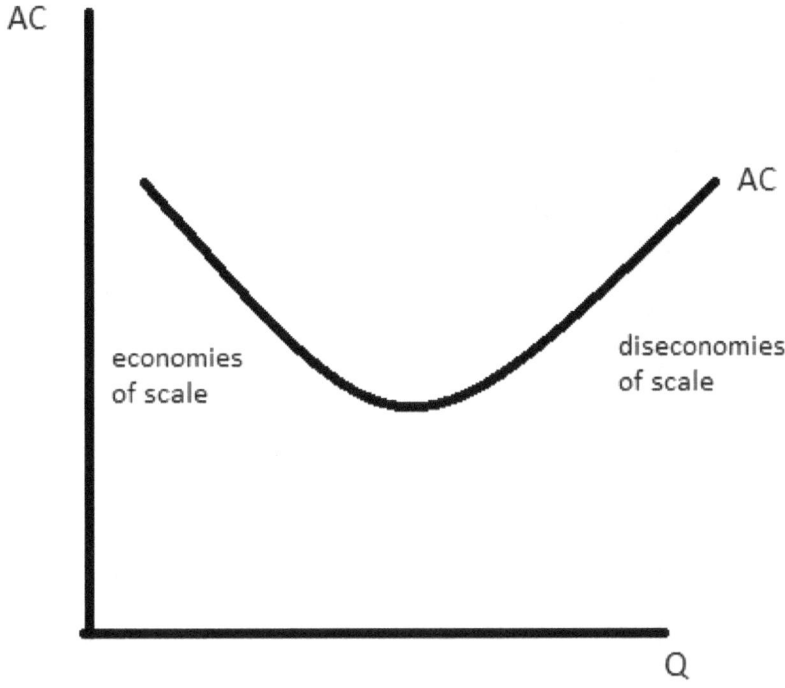

2. Diminishing returns is a so called short run phenomenon, meaning that it occupies usually a short time scale, where at least one factor of production is fixed. An example might be a school which can attract lots of students and teachers, but the building is too cramped to accommodate the growth in numbers. Planning permission may be hard to get, so in the short run, the firm has to suffer the consequences. This is where diminishing marginal returns occur. A classic example is a small plot of land in say Pakistan. It may be large enough to support three workers. However with each additional worker, the land is seen to be smaller and smaller in its economic ability to feed all the workers. The marginal product of the fourth worker

might be 3 units of produce, while the marginal product of the fifth worker might fall to 1 unit. With the addition of a sixth worker, the total product might fall, and the marginal product would be negative. The fundamental reason is that the size of the land is fixed, and this causes economic problems.

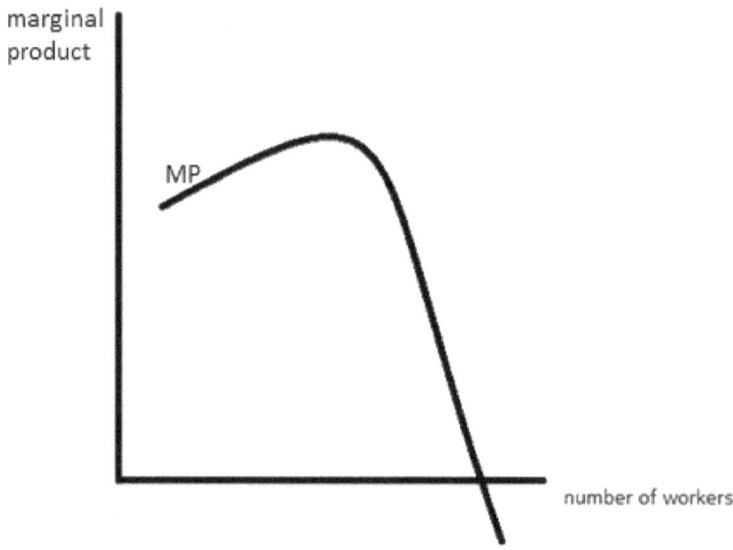

3. Decreasing returns to scale and diminishing marginal returns are best seen as two types of real life economic problem. The former is due to the firm growing too large, with spiralling diseconomies of scale causing average costs to rise sharply. The latter is due to the fact that at least one factor is fixed, and this causes business problems when it tries to grow.

AVERAGE AND MARGINAL REVENUE

1. Average revenue is the same as price. It is total revenue divided by output sold. The average revenue curve is the demand curve or price line. The marginal revenue curve is lower than the average revenue curve, because the marginal revenue curve plots the price at which the next unit is sold. To consider an example, at an output of 10 units, the price may be $5 a unit, yielding a total revenue of £50. The marginal revenue line shows the revenue earned from the next unit being sold, which might be $4. This concept is illustrated below.

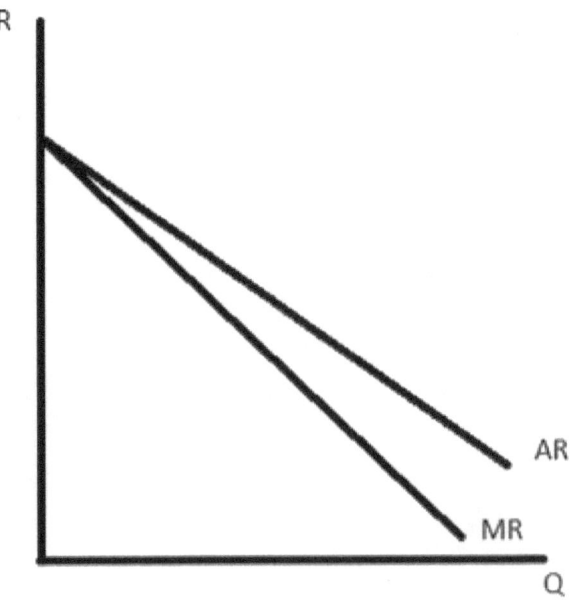

2. This idea might seem slightly counter-intuitive, so consider the following table, which effectively proves that the MR line is below the AR line.

Q	P (AR)	TR	MR
1	5	5	5
2	4	8	3
3	3	9	1
4	2	8	-1
5	1	5	-3

BREAK-EVEN POINT

1. If we examine the fixed cost and variable cost diagram, showing total costs, we can superimpose on this diagram a revenue line. The intersection point gives us the break-even point. The break-even point is where total costs are equal to total revenue. At a level of output greater than this point, the firm will start to make a profit, where total revenue exceeds total costs, while at an output level less than break-even, a loss will be incurred. This is a useful business tool for evaluating how many shoes or ships a firm has to make to break-even. The total costs will usually include the salary of the owner, so effectively the profit area is an area of abnormal profit, otherwise called economic rent or supernormal profit. (Incidentally, while the phrase "abnormal profit" usually means profit greater than normal profit, it could imply a loss).

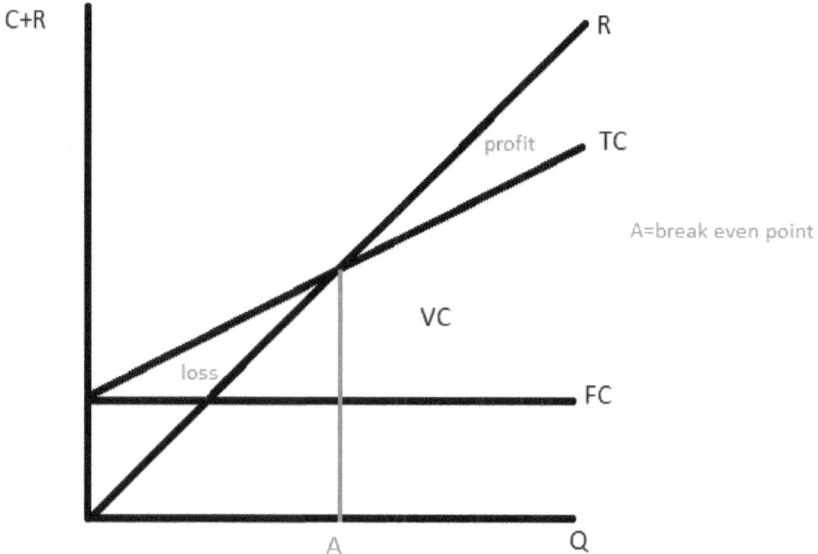

2. It is important to mention that in the short run a firm needs to cover only its variable costs to stay in business. The example which comes to mind is of a taxi driver. He has an incentive to get out of bed and drive during the day, searching for fares and revenue, if the income he earns exceeds the cost of petrol. However in the long term, he needs also to cover his fixed costs, such as the servicing costs of the vehicle, or a replacement vehicle. In the long run firms must earn normal profit to survive, and this means covering both fixed and variable costs.

OPPORTUNITY COST AND PRODUCTION POSSIBILITY CURVES

1. If a student decides to read an Economics book, rather than engaging in his second choice, watching a Hollywood DVD, he loses the opportunity to watch the DVD. This is the lost opportunity, known as the opportunity cost. Time and money can only be allocated or spent in one way or another; the same money cannot be spent twice. For example, the government of a country can either spend tax revenue on defence or education, the same tax money cannot be spent twice. The formal definition of an opportunity cost is "the next best opportunity forgone".

2. We all live in a world of choices and opportunity costs, and this concept has strong application in the field of production possibility curves or frontiers. A production possibility curve is a simplified version of a complex economy. We simplify the country, by assuming, for example, that it only produces manufactured secondary goods like cars and computers, and tertiary services like tourism, health care and education. The appropriate diagram is as follows.

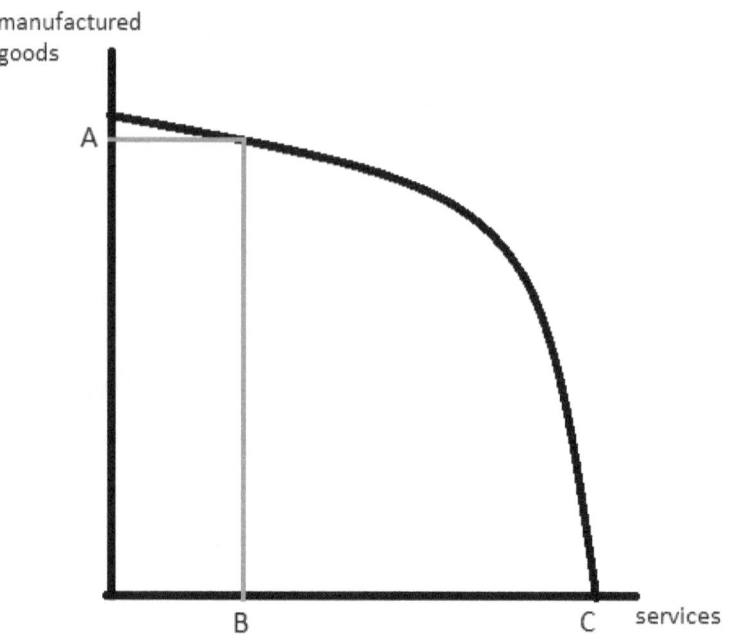

3. If we look carefully at the diagram, we can see that there is a choice about how many manufactured goods and services are produced and provided. If the economy allocates most of its economic resources to producing manufactured goods, there will be far fewer resources available for services. The effect of this is that a decision to produce mostly manufactured products, has a high opportunity cost in terms of services not provided. If quantity A of manufactured goods is created, there is a lost opportunity shown by BC.

4. Policy makers need to be acutely aware of the opportunity cost of their decisions. If money is spent in one direction, the same tax revenue is not available for

spending in a different direction. There is competition for scarce resources. Spending on health care means that there will be less funding for road building, missiles and social welfare.

5. Production possibility curves also have application to such matters as efficiency and economic growth. If an economy is producing at a point inside the curve, this means there is inefficiency due for example to misallocation of resources, high unemployment, or poor quality management. Output on the curve implies an efficient economy, and since no economy is wholly efficient, output de facto will always be at some point inside the curve. Some economies are more efficient than others, so Switzerland may be nearer the curve than Mozambique.

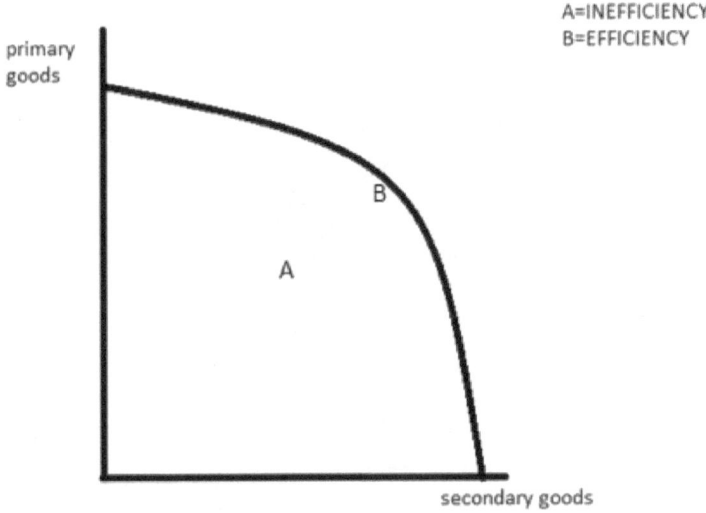

A=INEFFICIENCY
B=EFFICIENCY

primary goods

B

A

secondary goods

6. As an economy moves closer and closer to the frontier, this means economic growth is being achieved. Economic growth is when the nation's output is rising in total, and total national income is improving.

7. The phrase production possibility curve means that we are looking at the potential output and efficiency of a country. As a country strives to achieve growth, the productive potential will expand, and the curve will shift gradually to the right. As a country improves its efficiency and its output rises, the curve shifts outward, and one has the impression of a man reaching for an object which moves away from him as he reaches. This reflects the fact that no economy ever achieves complete efficiency, so as you move towards efficiency, the productive potential moves away from you and you never fully attain it.

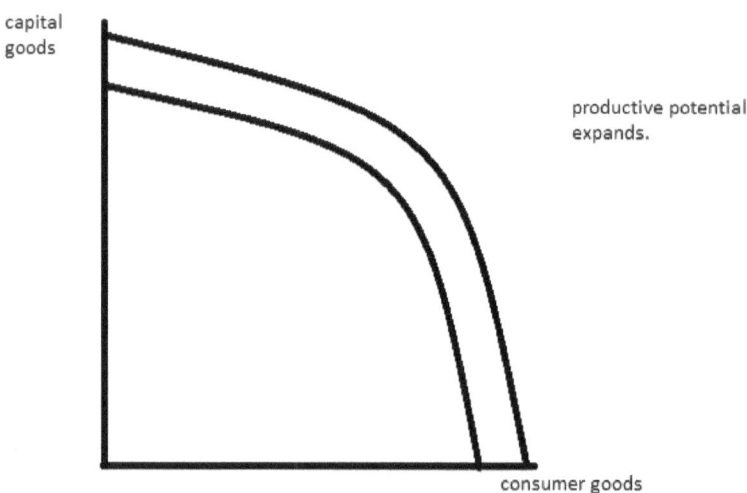

capital goods

productive potential expands.

consumer goods

8. The normal PPC is shaped in such a way as to indicate that as a country over-specialises on one group of products, in this case public goods, the opportunity cost rises. (A constant opportunity cost PPC would be a line with constant gradient, rather than a curve).

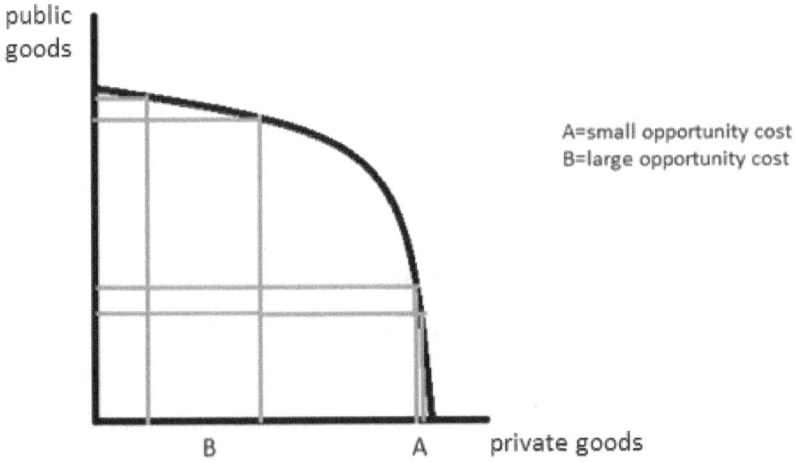

A=small opportunity cost
B=large opportunity cost

THE AIMS OF GOVERNMENT

1. Governments around the world have a range of common aims. We refer to governments within the enlightened world, because it is clear that governments in fascist or communistic countries may have their own perverse agendas. We refer to governments in the broad free market spectrum.

2. One central aim of government in the developed or less developed world, is to promote economic growth. Economic growth means increasing economic output. Gross domestic product is the most general term given to a country's economic product. GDP is the output of all the firms based in a country in one year. The GDP of the US is circa $17 trillion. A trillion is a thousand billion, and a billion is a thousand million. Increasing GDP is seen as being paramount in the free market, because it equates to rising income levels. This means that the average person will become wealthier. Obviously there are issues concerning the distribution of income, but growth is often seen as something which trickles wealth down to all sectors of society, given time.

3. Another aim of government is to reduce the level of unemployment. Unemployment is usually measured by the percentage of the workforce recorded unemployed to receive welfare benefits. Unemployment is a clear

cause of social inequality. Traditionally, unemployment in excess of 5% was seen as being an economic taboo, however since 2008 the ceiling on unemployment has been lifted. High levels of unemployment are likely to lead to deep-seated social problems. It must not be forgotten that National Socialism was largely a product of mass poverty and mass unemployment. Unemployment in countries like Spain and Greece is presently hovering around 25%, one quarter of the workforce. This creates the potential for violent social turmoil.

4. The aim or objective of low inflation is another commonly shared value of democratic governments. The reason is that inflation means rising prices, and if they rise too fast, it prejudices poorer people in society. They have to cope with rising prices, but often their income levels are fixed, as they do not have the power to demand higher wages.

5. Having a satisfactory balance of payments is a further aim of government. The balance of payments focuses largely on exports and imports. If a country is importing too much, but exporting little, gradually all the wealth gets squeezed out of the system. In economic parlance, we say that leakages exceed injections. A country which can export is a country which can grow wealthier. Recent examples would be Japan and Switzerland, whose rising income levels are due to strong export performance.

6. Governments aim to keep the budget deficit within manageable limits. A budget deficit arises when government spending exceeds tax revenue. It is now seen as a good thing to be willing to run a deficit, as this allows the level of total demand in a country to stay high, however there is consensus that excessive deficits can be damaging. The main reason for the negativity of huge deficits is that it means that government is borrowing large sums from inside and outside the country. In the end, most debts have to be repaid, with interest.

7. The maintenance of a strong and stable currency is another focus for governments around the world. The currency needs to be strong enough to afford vital imports like oil, but "weak" enough to facilitate exports. When there is disequilibrium in the exchange rate, then the economy will suffer. A recent case in point is the excessive appreciation of the Swiss franc, which threatens export revenue, as the country's exports are simply too expensive. This damages sales of exports like tourism, education and luxury watches.

8. A main aim of most civilized governments is the solution of the problems associated with market failure. Thus, governments need to address the issues of pollution, negative externalities, income inequality, consumer exploitation by imperfect competition, and the other items associated with market failure explained previously.

9. It needs to be mentioned that many governments around the world do not heed the significance of many of the classic aims of government. Their main aims focus on the propagation of a political agenda and the seizure of power and economic resources from the masses. We are, however, focusing on the aims and objectives of egalitarian democratic regimes.

THE COSTS OF UNEMPLOYMENT AND INFLATION

1. Unemployment has a range of very serious costs. At an individual, family and social level, unemployment increases the rate of depression, alcohol and drug abuse, family breakdown, violence and crime. These social costs are magnified by the socio-economic costs in the form of increased government spending on such areas as drug and alcohol addiction clinics, police, prisons and the legal system. The most serious cost is perhaps the economic cost. Unemployment causes recession, which means falling incomes and lower tax revenue. Unemployment means that the level of demand diminishes, which can result in falling total (aggregate) demand. This can prompt deflation, which means falling prices. When prices fall, consumers delay their purchases, setting in motion a further round of growing unemployment and deeper recession. From a government perspective, unemployment means less tax revenue, but more government spending on welfare, so a budget deficit results. This is where government spending exceeds tax revenue. This in turn results in spiralling debt, as the government borrows through selling bonds.

2. Inflation means rising prices. A rate of inflation of 3% means that prices are rising at 3% per year. High inflation (10%) damages poor consumers, because they

are often on a fixed income, and don't have the economic muscle to demand higher wages. The rich tend to get richer, as the poor get poorer. Wealthy people have assets such as land, houses or valuable paintings, which tend to become more expensive as inflation kicks in. The net result of the poor becoming poorer, and the rich becoming richer, is social division.

3. Inflation means that exports are expensive, and so export revenue declines. In time, inflation will damage and weaken the exchange rate, causing imports like oil to become too expensive. The current account of the balance of payments (export revenue and spending on imports) is likely to turn negative. The deficit will drain wealth from the country.

4. Inflation causes investment levels to fall, as few investors want to put money into a risky, inflation ridden country.

5. Inflation causes fiscal drag, meaning that wages rise, and people end up paying more in taxes. Some will be dragged up into a higher tax band.

6. Inflation causes unemployment. One reason is that firms' costs rise and they fire workers to keep costs down. Also, government and the central bank attack high inflation by high interest rates, high direct taxes and low levels of government spending. All of these approaches cause consumer spending and business

investment to fall. The decline in aggregate demand kills jobs.

7. The joint perils of high unemployment, traditionally above 5%, and high inflation (10%) must not be disregarded. We live in an era of low inflation, so we are somewhat blind to its perils. Unemployment on the other hand is everywhere to be seen; in countries like Spain and Greece it is 25% of the workforce. It must never be forgotten that National Socialism was the product of hyperinflation and mass unemployment in the 1920s and early 1930s. Hitler gained much support from the middle class who saw their savings destroyed by hyperinflation. This resulted in social division, where poor Germans looked with envy at rich, sometimes Jewish, entrepreneurs. The rest, as they say, is history.

TYPES OF UNEMPLOYMENT AND INFLATION

1. We have considered the costs of unemployment and inflation, but it is important to realise that there are many different types of unemployment, and more than one form of inflation.

2. Inflation can be due to too much demand, and this is known as demand-pull inflation. There may be too much consumer spending, or investment by firms, or government spending, or demand for exports. The other form of inflation is caused by rising costs and is known as cost-push inflation. This might be due to inefficiency, or low productivity, or costly imports. Demand-pull inflation is shown by the aggregate demand curve shifting right, while cost-push is shown by the aggregate supply curve shifting left.

DEMAND-PULL INFLATION

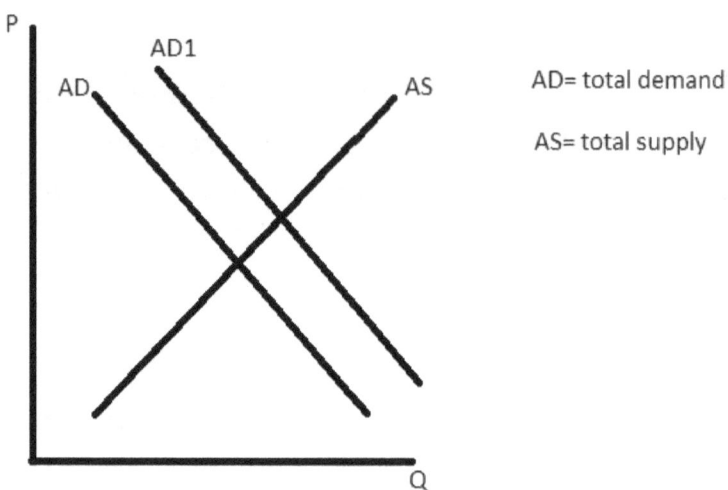

AD= total demand

AS= total supply

COST-PUSH INFLATION

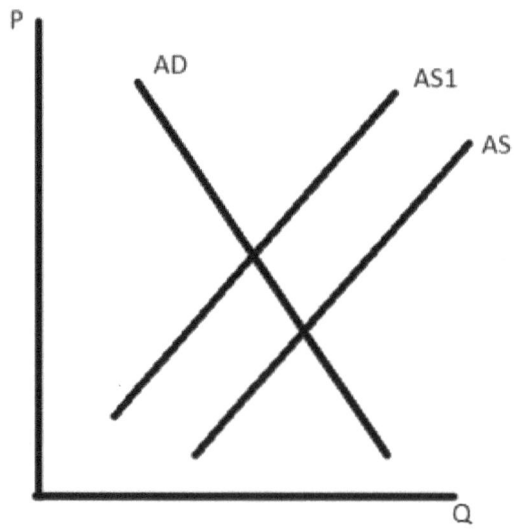

3. Unemployment may be cyclical unemployment due to lack of demand, or structural unemployment due say to the fact that a country's motor industry is not competitive with the Japanese. Frictional unemployment is job search unemployment, while seasonal unemployment might affect ski teachers in Austria. Residual unemployment refers to the unemployable minority, who lack the reliability to cope with regular employment.

4. Cyclical unemployment is also known as demand deficit unemployment, and this relates to the idea of the business cycle. The business cycle focuses on the idea that demand rises and falls. Demand grows under the influence of such factors as low interest rates, but this gradually causes inflation, and so interest rates rise, often causing a downturn or recession. The appropriate diagram is as follows.

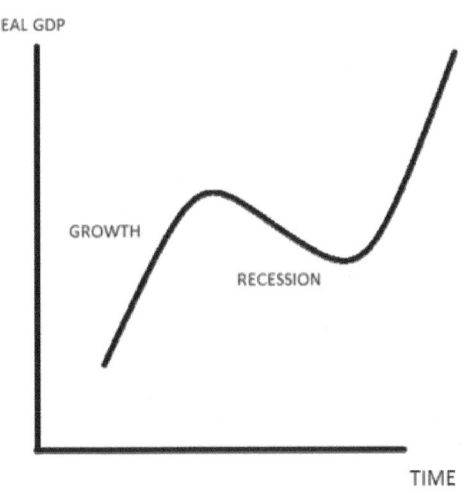

5. As we will shortly see in detail, high demand-pull inflation can be dealt with through such measures as higher interest rates to reduce consumption, while cost-push inflation can be moderated by improvements in productive efficiency. Demand deficit cyclical unemployment might require low taxes, high government spending and low interest rates, while structural unemployment depends, again, on efficiency improvements for its solution (known as supply side measures).

INFLATIONARY GAPS AND DEFLATIONARY GAPS

1. An inflationary gap is where there is too much demand in the economy, and this is causing a situation where there is no extra growth being created, but merely a rise in inflation. When an economy is at or near full capacity, then boosting demand will often simply cause prices to rise, as firms are unable to produce more goods to meet the market need. When an economy is operating near full capacity, this means that there will be low unemployment, and it is not easy to recruit workers. Also, capital machinery is working overtime. We can see on the next diagram, that lowering interest rates or direct taxes in this situation, would just cause inflation. Similarly, increasing government spending would have no positive effect on growth, but would prove to be merely inflationary. (Further explanation of this diagram will follow).

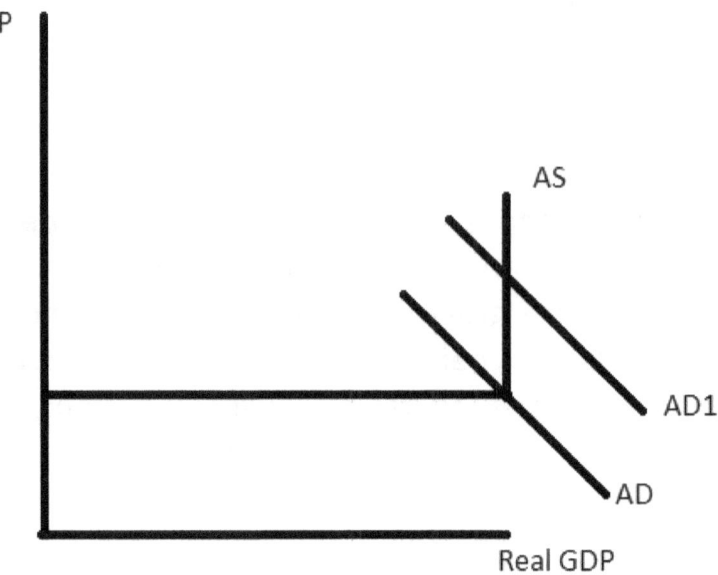

2. A deflationary gap arises when there is not enough
   demand in the economy. This is usually due to high
   unemployment. The lack of demand may cause prices
   to actually fall, (although falling prices are not
   illustrated on the following diagram). The following
   diagram shows a Keynesian version of reality, where
   there is insufficient demand; a deflationary gap. There
   is also an output gap, meaning that the economy is not
   operating at full capacity; it is capable of producing
   more than it is presently producing. There is
   equilibrium in the labour market, because demand
   meets supply, but this equilibrium is totally
   unsatisfactory, as the economy is tolerating very high
   levels of joblessness. During the great depression,
   unemployment was one quarter of the workforce. It is
   similar in Greece at the present time. In the 1920s

these problems led to extremist politics in Europe, and
today we see a somewhat similar scenario developing.

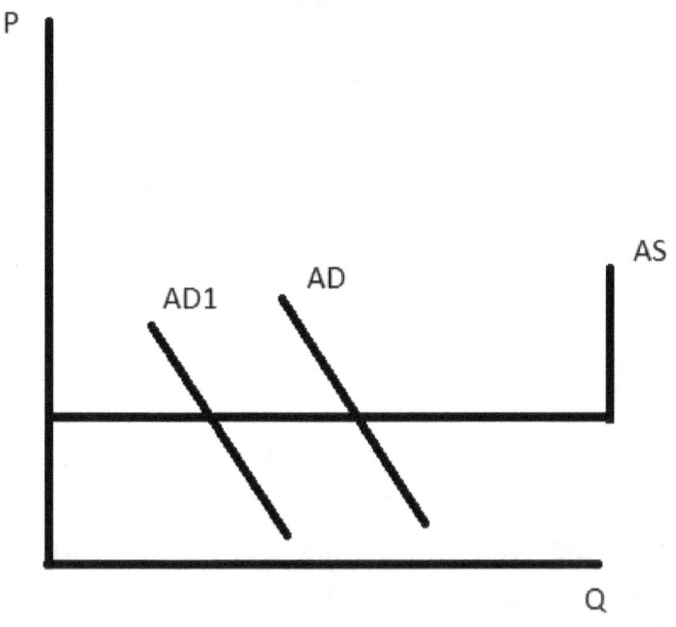

FISCAL POLICY

1. Governments can use fiscal policy to solve key economic problems, such as unemployment and inflation. Fiscal policy involves making changes to government spending, taxation and the budget. The idea is that government can increase aggregate demand in the economy by cutting taxes, and increasing government expenditure. This will often involve running a budget deficit, which is where government spending is greater than tax revenue.

2. Historically, it was seen as prudent to have a balanced budget, where government spending is equal to tax revenue. This was the status quo, except in times of war, when it was accepted that the government would have to spend a lot to finance conflict, during for example the Napoleonic wars.

3. In more recent times, governments around the world have become more comfortable with the idea of running a budget deficit, where spending exceeds revenue. The main reason for this change in approach, is the Great Depression in the 1930s, when governments in countries like the US came to accept that unless they tried to solve the problem of mass unemployment, there could be political revolution. Around the world fascist dictatorships were appearing, along with communist systems. Both of these

totalitarian models threatened the democratic free market model prevalent in the UK and the US. Leaders in democratic nations came to accept that running a deficit was more desirable than facing the risk of growing political unrest.

4. The influence of the famous economist Keynes also encouraged this move towards using high levels of government spending. Keynes published the celebrated book *The General Theory of Employment Interest and Money* in 1936. He argued convincingly that in times of high unemployment and economic peril, governments around the world had to be willing to interfere in the workings of the economy. Specifically they had to be willing to spend on public works to reduce unemployment. Public works could be anything from road or dam building, to the construction of new schools and hospitals. Anything to reduce the rate of unemployment could fall under the heading of public works. All sorts of cleaning and clearing projects could be financed by government to create jobs. Keynes made the point that the East End of London could be demolished and then rebuilt, as a public works programme designed to create jobs. He was only partly joking when he proposed this. He made the point that while it would be excellent for government to spend on worthwhile economic projects like social housing, anything which created jobs could be considered. There is reference to the idea of paying one group of people to bury bottles filled with money in fields, and then paying another group to go and search for the bottles.

Public works were mentioned as being similar to the building of the pyramids in ancient Egypt.

5. The combination of economic turmoil in the 1930s, coupled with the influence of Keynes, led to the New Deal approach in the US. This involved government spending huge amounts of money on public works projects like the Hoover dam. The aim was just to create jobs. This is the heart of fiscal policy to reduce unemployment. Government increases its expenditure, while simultaneously reducing taxes. The result is a deliberate budget deficit, where government spending perhaps greatly exceeds tax revenue. The resulting gap is filled by borrowing. Government borrows by selling government bonds. These bonds are very liquid, almost like cash, and can be easily sold on the stock market. The bonds can be sold by government to purchasers inside or outside the country. There has been concern in the US, about the quantity of bonds sold to China. When China buys US bonds, the dollar is strengthened, making Chinese exports to the US cheaper.

6. While Keynesian demand management has its critics, it should be noted that since 2008, governments around the world have been employing a Keynesian strategy to reduce mass unemployment. Politicians such as Obama in the US and Abe in Japan have been using this tactic.

7. Fiscal policy involves altering the level of government expenditure, and tax revenue and the deficit. Usually the aim is to promote growth through boosting job

creation. However, it is also possible to reduce government spending and increase income tax, thus running a budget surplus. This means that tax revenue exceeds spending. The net effect of this is to withdraw demand from the economy, and this is helpful if prices are rising too fast. Specifically, if the rate of inflation is too high, cutting government spending and increasing taxation, will reduce the level of consumption and investment in the economy, this causing prices to rise less quickly. (It should be noted that cutting indirect taxes is needed to reduce inflation, as indirect tax causes price rises).

8. When we examine the way fiscal policy works, it is possible to introduce the formula D=C+I. D stands for the total demand in the economy, which is a synonym of gross domestic product which represents the total output in one year. The word aggregate is often used as a synonym of total, and aggregate demand and supply are the usual terms. When there is a problem with unemployment, government runs a deficit, increasing its spending and cutting taxes. Jobs are created in say construction, and these workers earn money which they spend. This is consumption (C). Lower taxes further encourage consumption and investment (I) by business. The effect is a rise in demand, which should result in economic growth and job creation.

9. There is an interesting diagram which shows the way Keynesian demand management can create jobs. We see that total demand shifts to the right, moving along

the supply curve. Keynes envisaged the supply curve of the whole economy (aggregate supply) as being horizontal, when there is high unemployment, as there is no risk of inflation when so many people are in poverty and not spending. The boost of demand caused by the rising deficit causes job creation, and there is only a risk of fast rising prices, if this process is continued for too long.

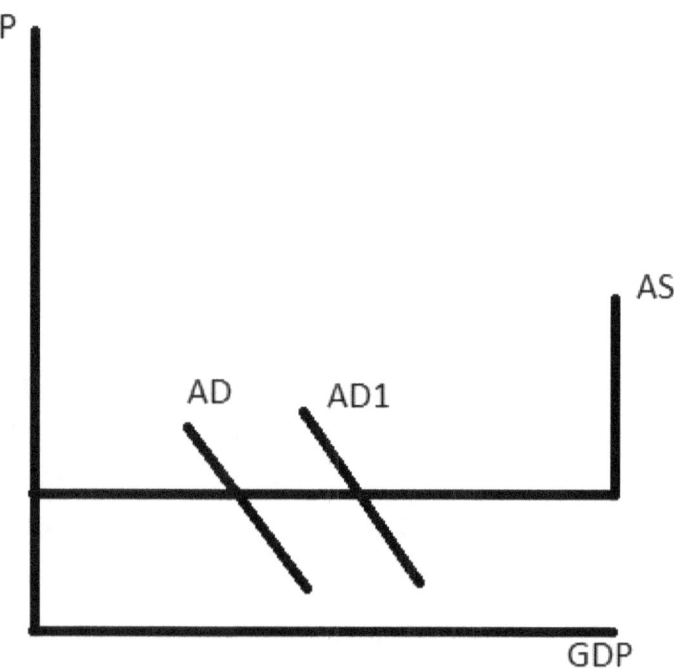

10. Critics of Keynesian policy point to the perils of running a high budget deficit on an ongoing basis. They also fear that all the "artificial" boosting of demand may cause fast inflation sooner or later. However, the consensus now is that all economic strategies need to be

employed when fighting the perils of mass unemployment. A budget deficit may not be a good thing, but high unsustainable unemployment is worse.

CROWDING OUT

1. One of the main criticisms of Keynesian Demand Management, which deserves special mention, is that it causes crowding out. The Keynesian approach to job creation is the deliberate running of a budget deficit, to keep aggregate demand high. This means that the government is required to finance the deficit through borrowing. If government spending is greater than tax revenue, the deficit must be filled by selling government bonds. One problem with this approach is that, if the government is borrowing all the available money, there will be less available for private firms and individuals to borrow. Firms will be crowded out. This means that there will be less private sector investment, as firms will have to pay a higher rate of interest to banks in order to borrow money. There might be higher levels of government spending, but this might be cancelled out to some measure, by the lower levels of investment by firms.

MONETARY POLICY

1. Governments can also employ monetary policy to solve economic problems. The role of monetary policy is usually allocated to the independent central bank, but in reality the central bank is an arm of government. It is independent only in the sense that it is not obliged to focus on winning the next election, and is thus to some measure immune from the problem of short term expediency. The central bank is thus free to focus on the key aims of government policy, namely economic growth, falling unemployment and controlling the rate of inflation.

2. The main tool or instrument of monetary policy in the modern age is interest rate changes. If there is a recession, with falling GDP and rising unemployment, the central bank will lower interest rates. The effect of this is that it will encourage borrowing and consumption. Firms will see a rise in consumers, as well as having themselves lower borrowing costs, and both these factors will fuel investment. As a result, demand, which is consumption and investment, will rise, and growth will pick up. Job creation also depends on exports, and lower interest rates often lead to lower exchange rates. This means that exports will be cheaper, and this should also create jobs. The reason the exchange rate falls when interest rates fall is that low interest is unappealing to overseas speculators

considering "investing" in a country. They will thus remove money from banks in the low interest rate country, moving it out of the country into another currency. For example, if the interest rate in the UK is 2%, but the interest rate in the US is 4%, Russian speculators will remove their hordes of sterling from UK banks, selling sterling on the foreign exchange market, and swapping it into dollars. As a result, the pound will lose value, as large quantities of it are being sold. This can be modelled as the supply curve of sterling shifting right, causing a price fall. The lower price of sterling means in turn that UK exports are cheaper, and this should increase export potential and revenue, for many goods and services like tourism.

3. So, when interest rates fall, consumption, investment and exports all increase. The longer formula which has the Keynesian stem is D=C+I+G+(X-M). Consumption is the man in the street spending. Investment means firms opening and expanding businesses, for example by building a new research facility or office block or factory complex. G stands for government spending, X represents exports, while M is for imports. Looking at imports, a lower exchange rate, caused by lower interest rates, will cause unnecessary imports to be too expensive, so consumers will purchase less. This should create economic growth inside the country, because importing causes a leakage of funds from the country, diminishing economic growth, especially if the imports are luxury imports. A lower sterling exchange rate means that luxury Swiss watches become prohibitively

expensive for marginal consumers. This bites especially on entry level luxury products like a basic Rolex. Purchasers of mega expensive timepieces are less affected by exchange rate variance.

4. The effect, therefore, of lowering interest rates is to promote economic revival and vitality through borrowing, consumption, investment and exports, while diminishing unnecessary luxury importing. One paradox with interest rates is that low interest rates often encourage consumers and businesses to borrow too much. When variable interest rates start to rise, the borrower is often unable to pay back the money due. This is a particular problem with mortgage purchases of houses. These purchases are often funded by a variable interest rate loan, and while it might be easy to repay when interest rates are modest, if they rise then it might become very hard for the borrower to repay. Rising interest rates usually occur to control inflation, which is often the result of dynamic growth. The result tends to be a scenario of boom and bust, when borrowing mounts under low interest rates, designed to create jobs. Then, as prices rise, interest rates are increased to discourage borrowing, but this causes a slump as borrowers default on their variable loans. Such was the scenario leading up to the sub-prime meltdown.

5. Monetary policy, as has been hinted at, is also employed to control the beast inflation. Inflation becomes very dangerous in its double digit form (above

10%). The reason is that it creates social division, with unskilled workers being unable to afford basic necessities. Also, as previously discussed, unemployment is fuelled through rising firms' costs and high interest rates.

6. When inflation is on the rise, the central bank will often pounce to decrease demand, thus reducing demand-pull inflation. They do this by increasing interest rates. Interest rates are usually changed by a small increment at a time, but the changes can be made every month, and before you know it, a 3% rate has become a punishing 7% rate. At the time of writing, interest rates are at an all-time low, as economies around the globe struggle to shake off the damage caused by the sub-prime fiasco. When interest rates rise steeply, consumption dramatically falls, as does investment. Demand for exports also declines, while imports may increase, due to the strengthening exchange rate. The effect is less demand and less demand-pull inflation. The diagram is shown below. Lower inflation means that prices are still rising, but more slowly than before. Most governments aim for inflation around 2%. The diagram is a two dimensional model of more complex reality, and the shift of the demand curve left, would in the first instance imply falling inflation rather than falling prices.

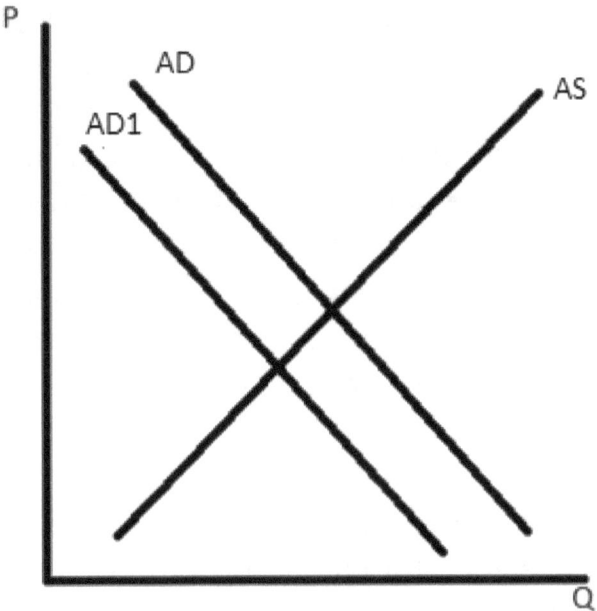

7. One needs to be aware, that while interest rate policy is the main tool of monetary policy, the central bank can also use other techniques to tame the economy. One recent development has been quantitative easing. This involves the central bank buying government bonds from banks, along with other securities like mortgage backed debt. The central bank pays a good price for the asset, and the cash paid improves the liquidity of the banking system. This means that banks have more cash to lend, and will lend it at a lower rate of interest due to the higher quantity available. In the UK the figure of £300bn represents the amount of quantitative easing presently operating. The process is often criticised as being the government "printing money". This is not

really accurate, it is more the central bank swapping one form of money for another. It is exchanging illiquid assets for cash; one form of "money" being exchanged for another. The verdict is still out on the merits of QE, but it has been an extensive experiment in extending the sphere of traditional monetary policy. One fear is that it simply stores up the potential for inflation in the future. Given high unemployment, there is little sign of an inflationary bubble, except maybe in some stock markets around the world.

8. One problem with both fiscal and monetary policy, is that they are good for combating either unemployment or inflation, but they are not good at fighting both at the same time. For example, low interest rates are great for creating jobs, but they are useless for dealing with inflation. At the present time, 2015, governments in the developed world in particular, are still running large budget deficits and having low interest rates, to create economic recovery.

SUPPLY SIDE ECONOMICS

1. We have explored the fact that fiscal and monetary policy are excellent instruments for tackling either inflation or unemployment. They are not perfect, in that their use during a downturn may cause excessive borrowing at an individual, business and governmental level, however they are universally applied with generally significant effect. However, they lack the capacity to control both inflation and growth simultaneously.

2. Supply side economics focuses not on influencing the demand side of the economy, but on activating supply through increased efficiency. Monetary and fiscal policy attempt to manipulate the aggregate demand curve, to create jobs or stifle inflation. Supply side policy puts more of a focus on improving the productive efficiency of the whole economy, or aspects of it. By improving productive efficiency, average costs fall, and the supply curve shifts to the right. This creates economic growth with lower inflation. The next diagram shows the twin benefits of shifting supply rather than demand. One of the fathers of supply side economics is Milton Friedman, who in such books as *Capitalism and Freedom* (1962), emphasised the need to control inefficient government activities.

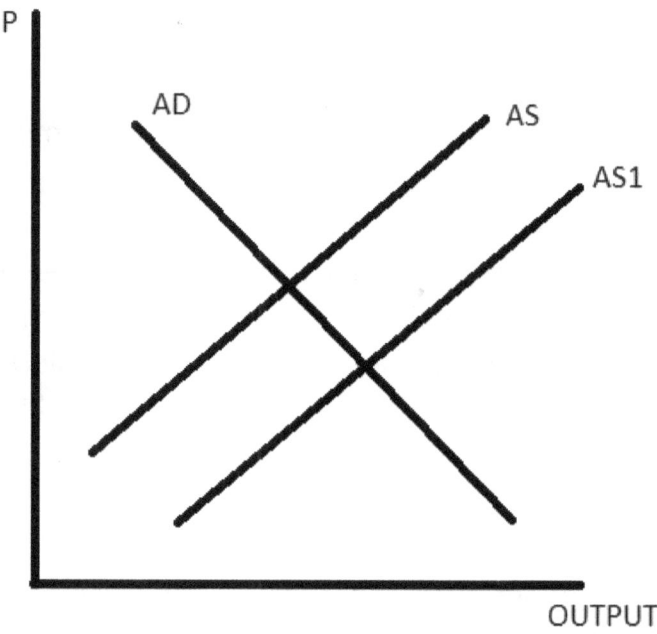

3. The supply side emphasis is on privatisation which will remove the role of the cumbersome state from business affairs. The government of a country has no incentive to run say a railway system efficiently, because they are using tax revenue to fund the project. Better to pass ownership to private firms who will strive to reduce average costs and improve efficiency. The privatisation experiment has been implemented in many countries, with somewhat mixed results. There is perhaps a measure of consensus that government is rather cumbersome in its operation of water, energy, telephones and other public utilities. However there is some scepticism about the high prices charged by the newly privatised firms. Government can get round this

problem by putting controls about how high the privatised monopolies can raise their prices. But the fact remains, they are monopolies, so the spectre of exploitation raises its ugly head.

4. Another supply side economic policy is deregulation. This is where unnecessary rules and regulations, which hinder business start-ups and business operation, are scrapped or minimised. The effect of cutting all the red tape is that businesses should start with increased frequency and rapidity. This ought to create jobs and prosperity for all. However, there have been some problems with deregulation, in that often the baby has been thrown out with the bathwater. By this I mean, that necessary rules and regulations have often been relaxed, along with the unnecessary rules. An example of this is the deregulation of the financial services industry, with the repeal of the Glass-Steagall Act in 1999. This made it possible for investment banks and high street banks to merge and blend. Often speculation ensued, with high street depositors finding that their hard earned savings were being lent to individuals who had no chance of ever repaying the mortgage loans. There were so called NINJA loans. Loans to people with no incomes, jobs or assets. However, despite the problems, Friedman makes a most compelling case when he argues that markets can often best regulate themselves. The market communicates information more rapidly and efficiently than a government bureaucrat.

5. A further supply side measure is the introduction of tax incentives. The idea is that high taxes punish enterprise, and perhaps the biggest offender is progressive income tax. A lower tax for all is seen as a way of revitalising a dormant economy. The Laffer curve provides some support for this idea. It suggests that as the rate of taxation falls, tax revenue may actually rise, due to the very fast economic growth rate. In spite of the lower rate of taxation, revenue might increase. This is all based on the assumption that tax rates are too high in a given situation. The critique of this position is that low income tax, for example 15% for all, just rewards the wealthy.

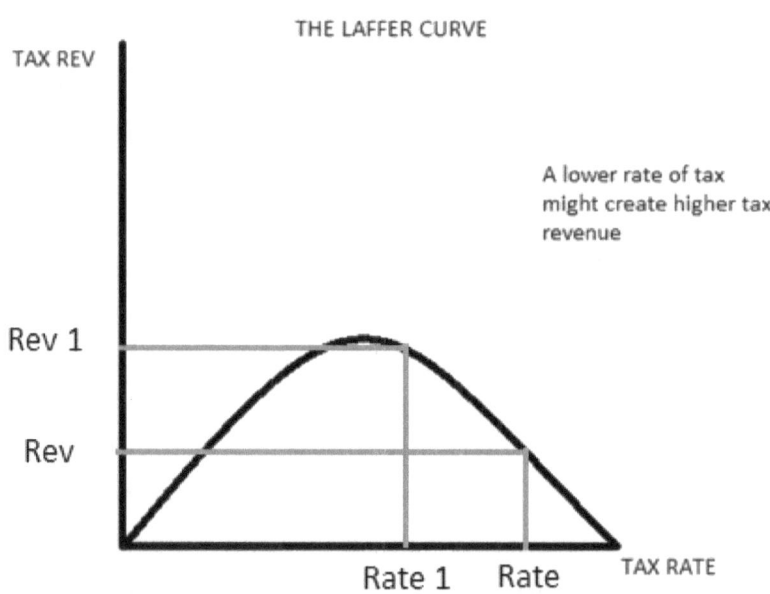

THE LAFFER CURVE

TAX REV

A lower rate of tax might create higher tax revenue

Rev 1

Rev

Rate 1   Rate   TAX RATE

6. A favourite supply side innovation is to make the labour market a lot more flexible. A flexible labour market implies many things, for example it means that minimum wages should be removed. This means that a worker will get the equilibrium wage he deserves in the free market, not some higher government protected wage level. The rationale behind the elimination of minimum wage legislation, is that a high minimum wage actually causes job losses. We can see this idea on the following diagram. At the artificially high minimum wage, the quantity demanded of workers is much lower than the quantity supplied, and somewhat lower than the market equilibrium. This means that the very people government seeks to help, will be the first to lose their jobs, as they are unskilled and from the firm's profit-maximising perspective, not worth the money.

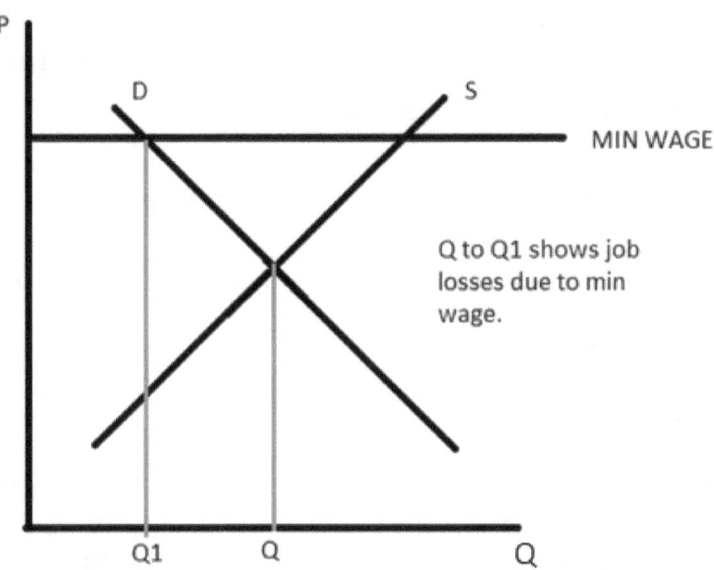

7. The flexible labour market also means that it should be easy to hire and fire workers, and short term contracting should be allowed. The logic is that it will encourage firms to hire more workers. If you cannot fire a worker, you have an incentive to not hire him in the first place. In some countries certain employees have a job for life, irrespective of how much or how little true competence they may possess. Education jobs in the UK are one example. However, obviously a culture of short term contracts, sometimes with zero hours, is open to abuse.

8. Flexible labour means giving females and ethnic minorities' equality of opportunity. The concept is to have an excellent woman rather than a second rate man in a post. It is difficult to criticise this idea, but there are possible costs even here. For instance a right to work may become an obligation in cultural terms; one cost is that women feel obliged to work, and their children may receive less care.

9. A flexible labour market means that excessive trade union power should be liquidated. The Thatcher government in the UK in the 1980s was one of the first to attack excessive union power. Excessive power means that wages are too high, there are frequent strikes, and the economy loses output. Previously this attack on organised labour had also been conducted in Chile and Argentina, with extreme brutality, but many now take the view that Thatcher paved the way for

economic progress through improved efficiency in this regard.

10. Supply side also appreciates the importance of new technology, education and training, and any policy moves to speed up the efficiency of a moribund economy.

THE CIRCULAR FLOW OF INCOME

1. A key macroeconomic device is the circular flow of income. This concept was given physical shape by Phillips at the London School of Economics, when he built a physical model of the flow of income in an economy.

2. The circular flow of income purports to show how money flows in a circular fashion around an economy. For example I will earn a salary, but this will mostly be spent on rent, shopping for groceries, luxury spending and pocket money for one's children. Money is rarely if ever stationary, it is mostly on the move, travelling from point A to point B. Even when money appears to be stationary and dormant, as when it is in a bank account, actually this sum is used as the basis of other people's borrowing and spending, as banks need a certain amount of deposited money, before they are permitted to lend.

3. The circular flow of income depicts how income is earned and then consumed. This is the main dynamic of the circular flow, in a so called closed economy. But in reality an economy is not closed from other influences. An economy is not only earning an income and then spending it. Some of it is saved, and some of it is taxed, and some of it might be spent on imports. These three items, saving, taxation and imports, are called leakages

from the economy. The reason is that in excess each can be damaging to economic growth and revival. If a country imports an excessive amount of unnecessary luxury goods, this is a drain on a country's prosperity, as money is quite literally leaking out of the country. The money paid for a German BMW or a Swiss Omega or a holiday in Jamaica, are all funds streaming from a country. Instead of spending inside the country, money is leaking out like a dripping tap. It is, of course, perfectly acceptable to spend on essential imports such as oil and other raw materials, and there is no entitlement to reduce consumer preference by prohibiting imports in general, but in the US for example, there has been a current account deficit this month of some $50bn. This means that imports are greater than exports by this amount. A leakage from the economy indeed!

4. Saving is also essential, otherwise there is no money available for banks to lend. However, excessive saving means that money is not being consumed in spending, and this is bad for the level of aggregate demand, growth and jobs. Japan is to some extent a country of savers, and this conservatism is one reason for the lethargy of the Japanese economy. Japan has been teetering on the brink of recession and deflation (falling prices) for many years and even decades. While saving is good, excessive saving can paralyse an economy.

5. The idea of taxation being a leakage needs little explanation. We all feel that taxes are too high, and

that inefficient and even sometimes corrupt government, fritters away our hard earned cash. Everyone accepts that some measure of taxation is required, to provide basic public goods, but when government spending consumes nearly 50% of GDP this is surely excessive. Friedman has made the point that government became, after the Second World War, a giant behemoth which threatened, and still threatens, to overwhelm the general populace. The aim of supply side economics is to reduce the role of government to the provision of only the most basic public goods, such as a legal system and a defence force.

6. The notion that excessive saving, importation and taxes, are somehow detrimental to national prosperity, will meet with approval from most thinking people. However, there are another group of forces, called injections, which are seen generally to be beneficial for an economy. We can now examine the positive role of the three injections into the economy.

7. The first injection is exports. A country which exports is on the road to prosperity. This is evident from a casual glance at the role of exports in Switzerland, Japan and Saudi Arabia. In each of these destinations, exportation has caused the growth of prosperity. It matters not if the exports are ski vacations, chocolate, luxury watches, motorcycles, cars, computers or crude oil. Either way this creates injections of prosperity in the long term into the country concerned. Countries such as Japan can easily rack up a current account surplus of

$200bn a year. This is the excess of exports over imports, and constitutes an injection into the circular flow of income. Japan has not one drop of its own oil, yet prosperity since the 1940s is due largely to exports.

8. We can consider the role of government spending. According to Keynes, high levels of government spending are essential during a serious downturn, to deliver economic revival. If there is a recession, or even a threat thereof, Keynes proposed that government should pump up the level of total demand, to ensure low unemployment. The creation of wealth through running a budget deficit may seem strange to some, but it has often produced strong results. If governments around the globe did not embark of Keynesian demand management in 2008, it seems correct to say that economies might well have had to endure a longer economic downturn. No one is saying that living on debt is a good thing, but a budget deficit, even a sizeable one, might be better than the torment of rising unemployment. It might be the lesser evil, at least this is the view of such renowned economists as Krugman. It is fair and correct to say that there is no absolute agreement on the correctness of using a Keynesian strategy of high spending on public works, but to many it is seen as an important injection into the circular flow. Others point to the fact that using these policies at the wrong time, can be inflationary. This proved to be the case by the 1970s, when the British Prime Minister James Callaghan gave his famous speech in the House of Commons, explaining that excessive and

unjustified government spending had to be curtailed, as all it was doing was creating a spiral of inflation, without reducing the rate of unemployment in the long term.

9. The final injection into the circular flow, will cause little debate in terms of its validity. If the government can adopt policies which encourage and facilitate investment, this investment will be good for economic growth. Investment is when a firm opens or expands, and the job creation flowing from this is self-evident.

10. The diagram below shows that when injections like investment and exports, are greater than leakages such as excessive importation and high taxes, then an economy will grow steadily. Any government policies which facilitate injections, for instance tax breaks on investment, or promoting exports, while reducing excessive taxes, will be beneficial for the country as a whole.

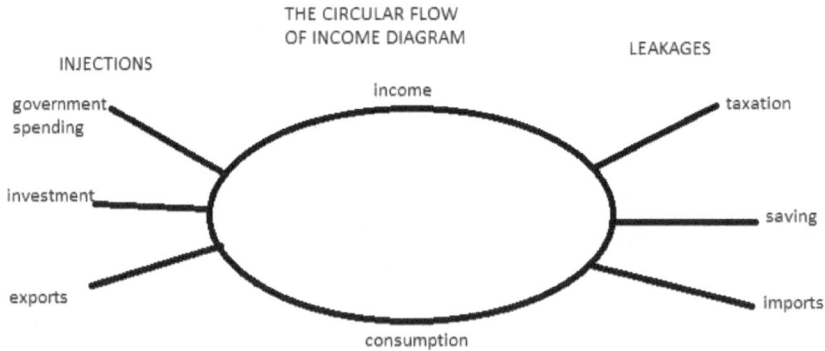

THE CIRCULAR FLOW
OF INCOME DIAGRAM

INJECTIONS

LEAKAGES

government
spending

income

taxation

investment

saving

exports

imports

consumption

THE MULTIPLIER

1. Acutely connected to the circular flow diagram, is the Keynesian concept of the multiplier. The multiplier was introduced by Keynes in his 1936 book, *The General Theory*. It should be remembered that Keynes was a mathematician before turning to Economics, under the influence of his teacher Alfred Marshall. This point is worth mentioning, because Keynes, like Marshall, was keen to introduce a measure of mathematical rigour to the discipline of Economics.

2. The concept of the Keynesian multiplier, is a mathematically based idea. It uses the concept of an infinite geometric series, to model the way investments and other injections into the circular flow might work. An example of a geometric sequence would be 16,8,4,2... To find r, the common ratio, you divide the second term by the first, which gives a value of 0.5. The series is the sum of these geometric terms to infinity. The formula for an infinite geometric series is that the sum of the series is equal to the initial term divided by 1 minus the common ratio. In our example, the sum would be 32, which is 16 divided by 0.5. This is expressed as follows: -

$$S = \frac{u1}{1-r}$$

3. What is the significance of this formula for the economic world? Well the idea is that the $u1$ stands for the initial injection into the economy, for example an increase in government spending on public works projects. The total beneficial effect of this injection is the injection divided by 1 minus the r value, and this r value is called by Keynes, the marginal propensity to consume (MPC). This is basically the percentage of one's extra income one spends. It can now be exemplified, to see exactly how Keynes thought this might work.

4. Consider the Keynesian formula, based on the infinite geometric series formula. His version would be $M = \dfrac{1}{1 - mpc}$. If people spend on average 80% of their extra income, then the MPC is 0.8. This means that the Keynesian multiplier effect is 1 divided by 1 minus 0.8, which is 1 divided by 0.2, which gives an M value of 5. This suggests, according to a Keynesian version of reality, that an increase in government spending of some £1m might boost GDP by £5m, a multiplier effect of 5. (An alternative formula is 1 divided by MPS+MPT+MPM; marginal propensity to save, tax and import).

5. It is arguable to what extent it is valid to assume that an economy works like a geometric series, but if it does, Keynes has a powerful argument. There is criticism in spades from Milton Friedman in his 1962 book, *Capitalism and Freedom*. Friedman, a Nobel Prize

winning economist, claimed that there was little de facto evidence that could be found by him, of any multiplier effect whatsoever. Friedman had paradoxically a lot of respect for Keynes as an economic thinker, but he was hostile to ideas which led to an increased role for government. The Keynesian vision of reality is one which permits the intercession of government into markets. This, Friedman claims, has led to the growth of big powerful government, to the deficit of the individual. The most obvious exemplar of this is high taxes, sometimes referred to by Friedman as "taxation without representation".

6. The multiplier idea can be envisaged from another perspective. It can be seen through the idea that money is a creative force. If a business person successfully starts a firm with £1m, it does not seem unreasonable that the firm should generate wealth in excess of the initial injection. It would not be surprising if the firm's value was £5m after a few successful years. Another way of supporting the multiplier idea is to see the initial injection as like the raw materials used by an artist; the canvas, paint, linseed and brushes, along, of course, with the artist's time and labour. There can be no doubt that a finished work of art by Rembrandt is worth more than the initial ingredients used by him to construct the picture.

7. Whether one envisages the multiplier effect through the prism of a mathematical model or a metaphor about artists, or from the viewpoint of business

acumen, there is no doubt that the idea must be taken with some measure of seriousness, perhaps combined with a degree of critical reflection as to its validity.

8. A connected idea is the idea of the accelerator. This is the proposition that a 1% increase in demand will cause more than a 1% rise in investment. The logic is that as demand rises like a tide, firms are obliged to make larger lumps of investment. An example might be when a motorbike seller sees rising demand for his product. At some point he has to order in a range of new stock. The rising tide creates a large act of investment, with the former being somewhat smaller than the latter.

9. The combination of multiplier and accelerator builds on the circular flow, and it is often called the multiplier-accelerator.

10. When we examine our preliminary excursion into macroeconomics, we see that most civilized governments share the same basic aims of creating jobs and taming inflation, and they have fiscal, monetary and supply side tools at their disposal. The circular flow blends the ideas further together. Any policy move, for example lowering interest rates, or boosting direct taxes, will have implications from the perspective of the circular flow and the multiplier. One example might be that a cut in the interest rate would facilitate further investment, which would have a strong multiplier effect, creating growth of GDP. The MPC depends on how confident consumers are about the economy. Low

interest rates would generally increase that confidence, supporting a high MPC value and a corresponding high multiplier effect. However, high taxes would deplete confidence and the MPC would shrivel up, having a damaging effect on the multiplier-accelerator process. The term "macroeconomics" just means the big picture, looking at the whole economy and considering such key issues as unemployment, growth and inflation. "Microeconomics" relates to the world of individual firms, demand and supply, elasticity and costs.

THE GREAT DEBATE

1. There is a great debate between two main groups of economists, on the best approach to solving economic problems like unemployment, inflation and economic growth rates. The great debate is between Keynesian economists on the one hand and so called new classical economists on the other.

2. Keynesian economists are followers of the celebrated economist John Maynard Keynes, who revolutionised economic theory with his 1936 tome, *The General Theory*. This book is not a read for the general populace, but was designed by an economist for economists. However, close reading of key areas is quite possible by a student, and its purchase is recommended. Keynes argued that when the economy is in trouble, due to impending recession and high rising unemployment, the key approach is that government and the central bank have got to be willing to get involved to pump up demand as needed. The main idea is that government spending must rise as required, running the inevitable budget deficit, as taxes should also be lowered. The extra government expenditure on public works projects such as building dams and roads and improving infrastructure, will create jobs automatically. The jobs will be centrally in the lower skilled areas of the economy, for example labourers,

who are often the first to lose their jobs during a recession.

3. The concept of public works spending is still alive and well around the world, with Japan being one of the latest countries to spend on regenerating infrastructure, after natural disasters. Around $100bn has recently been allocated to this public works project, in an attempt to kick-start the economy, in order to ensure that Japan does not hover endlessly on the brink of recession.

4. The Keynesian approach was employed in the US in the 1930s, by Roosevelt during the New Deal years, however it is not clear if he was influenced directly by Keynes. It is more probable that the theory and the practice coincided on a basis of economic necessity. Often intellectual ideas are implemented when the reality of life finds them supportive and desirable. It needs to be perhaps mentioned that the US did not fully recover from the 1929 stock market crash, until government spending expanded in the lead up to the war years, and to a certain extent the jury is still out on the Keynesian case.

5. What is clear is that a Keynesian approach led to the expansion of the role of government, and it is this which caused the counter argument to be developed. The opposition view started in the University of Chicago, and the main proponent of the case against Keynes, was developed by Milton Friedman, in such

books as the 1962, *Capitalism and Freedom*. He argues against every element of Keynesian demand management, saying that there is little or no proof that meddling by government in the economy solves problems. He argues that the vast expansion of the role of government since the Second World War, is largely attributable to the influence of Keynesian economic policies. GDP is the output of all the firms based in a country in one year, and the expansion of government has meant that as much as 50% of GDP is down to government spending and its role in the economy. Friedman felt that there is a sort of zero sum game at play here; as the role of government increases, the role of the free market declines. He argues that free markets are far more efficient and dynamic than the non-incentivised moribund government apparatus. In his television series and book *Free to Choose* (1980), he illustrates many examples of how markets can perform apparent miracles, due to the magic of the price system, and the miraculous way it transmits information amongst participants in the economic system.

6. Friedman argues quite convincingly, that intervention in the economy tends to cause more problems than it solves. He builds on the key insights of Hayek, who in his seminal work, *The Road to Serfdom* (1944), illustrates quite convincingly that governments can't possibly have all the required information to make correct decisions about economic planning. The price system is like a vast brain stem, and the neurones of

the price mechanism have grown gradually through time. A small group of bureaucrats cannot have access to all the data required to correctly apply economic planning and policy. Friedman and Hayek argue that attempts at regulating the level of aggregate demand are bound to fail as all the required information is not available to any single small group of individuals. The collapse of the communist/socialist experiment in the Soviet Union tends to confirm the inferiority of central planning in comparison to free markets. There was a shortage of basic economic goods, both in quantity and quality, with non-availability of basic food like fruit, and quality motor vehicles. The vast diseconomies of scale of the Soviet experiment were in stark contrast to the efficiencies created by competition and the perfect competition model.

7. The great debate is far from over. The Chicago school proposed a whole raft of alternative policies, with Friedman focusing on the careful use of interest rates as a good way to create economic growth. The Chicago boys, as they were known, applied the raft of supply side ideas to countries like Chile and Argentina, with mixed success, before the big experiment in the UK and the US by Reagan and Thatcher in the 1980s. This was the first break with the dogma of Keynesianism, with governments embarking on wholesale privatisation and liberalisation and deregulation in every sphere of life, ranging from railways to the financial system. The result is the new world of neoclassicism, where we are, in a sense, back with the ideas of our economic

forefathers like Adam Smith. In *The Wealth of Nations* (1776), Smith made it clear that government should have a modest role to play in the economy, leaving most economic activity to the free market. Smith defined the role of the state in minimalistic terms, as a provider of basic education, defence, and the security of contracts through a reliable legal system. He focused on incentives, and illustrated the way lecturers in his university had been negligent due to lack of fear of losing their jobs. The free market approach of the economic grandfather Smith, so called classical economics, prevailed until the Keynesian revolution. With the impact of Friedman's ideas, the revival of classical economics took place, called new classical economics.

8. There are presently two groups of economic thinkers, centred in certain universities; those who still cling to the tenets of Keynesianism, and those who reject the role of government as a public works provider. The great debate continues, but since 2008, there has been more of a concurrence among politicians. Successful politicians, forever and always pragmatic, have borrowed ideas from the Keynesian school and from new classical economics. Any policies which work, or at least can be sold to the electorate as working, have been used. The desire to get re-elected has sometimes clearly been paramount, however many politicians do perhaps want to solve problems and improve people's lives, and they have used all available approaches to try and create jobs.

9. It is important to mention at this juncture, that there is a difference in economics between positive and normative economic statements. A positive economic statement is something which can be proved true or false. For example we can easily check if inflation has fallen from 4% to 2% over a certain 2 year period, in a specific country. We are unable to prove the statement that it is better to spend money on defence rather than education; that may be the opinion of some, but we cannot prove or disprove it. This is a normative statement. This distinction is applicable to the conflict between the Keynesian and the new classical approach to solving economic problems. Both schools of thought have their positions, and their arguments. Some of the arguments are intricate and plausible, by that falls somewhat short of an actual factual proof.

GROSS DOMESTIC PRODUCT, GROSS NATIONAL PRODUCT AND NATIONAL INCOME

1. There is a slight difference in economics between GDP, GNP, and NI. Gross domestic product is the basic term used by economists and government officials, to refer to the output of all the firms based in a country in one year. The world's largest economy is the US, with an output of circa $17tn. China and Japan and Germany follow in terms of total output. The location of the firms is the key measurement, not ownership, and we are looking at all the primary, secondary and tertiary goods and services.

2. GDP can be measured by looking at all the output of a country, or all the income earned from these products, or all the expenditure on these products. The figures should be the same, subject to minor alterations. There are thus three ways of measuring GDP; the output method, the income method and the expenditure method. One point which is rather meaningful, is the fact that goods must not be double counted, for example one must be careful not to measure the value of a rubber tyre on its own, and then include it again when one looks at the value of the finished motorcar.

3. GNP is often very similar, but it is slightly different in that it looks at ownership rather than just location.

(GNP is sometimes now called gross national income). So GDP will simply measure the value of the products of all the firms based in say Norway, irrespective of who owns the business, while GNP will investigate who owns the firm. Thus an adjustment must be made, to exclude the products created by firms owned by non-Norwegian citizens in Norway, and to add the value of products created by Norwegians based outside Norway, for instance a Norwegian firm in Chile. This adjustment is called net property income from abroad. Often the GNP of wealthy countries will be greater that their GDP, because of the fact that their citizens have invested overseas. In contrast, the GNP of developing economies might be less that their GDP, as many of the firms in say Nigeria, are owned by foreign investors in the oil industry.

4. National Income is GNP subject to an adjustment for depreciation of capital stock. Capital goods are goods which make other goods, like machinery. As these items slowly wear out, and are essential for the maintenance of levels of output, they need to be slowly replaced, and a sum is deducted from GNP to allow for this.

5. As we move on, it should be clear that GDP per person (per capita) is a much more meaningful figure than just basic GDP. This involves simply dividing the GDP by the population, to get an average income level. The size of GDP is semi-meaningless, because the wealth of the individual depends also on population size.

6. A last adjustment needs to be made. GDP can either be nominal or real. Nominal is then we look at the figure, before adjustment for inflation. Inflation is just rising prices. If we do not make this final adjustment, a country experiencing hyperinflation would appear to be growing massively. The idea of making GDP real, means we are removing price rises, inflation, from the calculation, to see by how much the economy has really grown in a year. GDP growth figures of 3% or 4% are seen as being impressive in the developed world, while fast growing developing economies may manage a rate of growth per annum of perhaps 8%. Inflation of above 2% is seen as dangerous. A little inflation can be a good thing, as it encourages consumers to keep spending before prices rise.

7. The gross national (or domestic) product deflator is another term for removing inflation to find real growth.

8. Thought about deflation is also merited. Deflation means falling prices, and this can be very dangerous as falling prices encourage consumers to delay spending, and the fall in demand can easily cause a recession with rising unemployment. Japan has been in and out of deflation for several decades, since the property and stock market crash of 1990. If there is deflation, the real GDP would have to be amended upwards, to take account of falling prices.

TO WHAT EXTENT IS REAL GDP PER CAPITA A GOOD MEASURE OF LIVING STANDARDS?

1. The traditional way of measuring and comparing living standards is to use real GDP per capita. For example if the GDP per person in Greece were to be lower than in Hungary, it would be assumed that people in Hungary have higher "living standards" and a better quality of life.

2. In fairly recent years the assumption that higher real GDP per person equates to a better standard of life has been seriously questioned. One obvious reason has been the widespread development of extreme pollution in some Asian countries. What is the point of having a few dollars more in your pocket, if you cannot breathe the air around you? Figures for China are especially worrying, with many large cities having pollution levels in the danger zone on a regular basis. The prevalence of high pollution levels means that using GDP is no longer a sufficient way of evaluating living standards.

3. There are other serious problems with using GDP as a measure of the quality of life. One problem is that GDP per capita gives an average measurement, and in nearly all countries, there is unequal income and wealth distribution. This means that the GDP figures can be very misleading, and in some cases quite meaningless.

There are ways of measuring inequality of income distribution, and the main one is the Gini coefficient, which provides a figure of between zero and one for a country. If an economy has a figure of one, it would mean that all the income is owned by one person or family. This is not far from the truth in some dictatorships like North Korea. In any case, rabid inequalities of wealth and income distribution greatly undermine the value of the GDP per person figures.

4. Another problem is that prices differ in different countries. A dollar will go much further in Angola than it will in England. As prices vary so widely, the real GDP figures, which are adjusted for inflation not prices, tend to lose validity and accuracy.

5. Another key issue is the government provision, or not, of merit and public goods. If the government provides health care and education to its citizens, then this is terribly important for living standards. GDP figures don't reveal this.

6. A connected issue is the rate of taxation in a country. If taxes are high, then the net income will be much less. Some economies have tax rates of 40% or above, while some income earners pay no tax in countries like Saudi Arabia (e.g. overseas teachers).

7. The life expectancy of citizens is also obviously very meaningful and this tends to bring us full circle to the

levels of pollution and the quality of government provision of merit and public goods.

8. One can go further and investigate lifestyle issues. One must look at what a person has to do to earn a certain income. One worker may have to live in a compound in Saudi Arabia, or another may have to drive 2 hours to work, while another may have a 5 minute amble along a country pathway. All of these factors bear on quality of life or living standards. In some countries people have the possibility of gaining success based on hard work and enterprise, while in others it is only wealth and privilege which can produce these opportunities. Some countries allow for the possibility of university education and the consequent personal and career growth, while in others only a very select minority are allowed such entry. All of the above factors, and many more, can have a bearing on living standards, so GDP is seriously flawed as a measure. However, its survival is due to the fact that it is a method of measuring used and agreed by all, or nearly all nations, and it is relatively simple to employ. It is also, in many cases, quite accurate as a measurement of living standards for the majority of the population. However, dissatisfaction with GDP as a measuring tool, has led to other approaches, and the most significant of these is called the Human Development Index.

9. The Human Development Index is an alternative to using real GDP per capita as a measurement of what living standards are actually like in a country. The HDI

does not reject GDP, but hopes to build upon it. It was largely the work of the Indian economist Sen, who felt that real GDP did not truly capture what was going on in the reality of Indian society. He proposed a system, which can now be briefly summarised.

10. There as three prongs to the HDI measurement. One dimension is to use the real GDP figure per person, but to adjust it for prices. This is called adjusting for purchasing power parity (PPP). The second aspect is to look at how long on average people live. The third aspect of HDI focuses on education, and how many years of education, on average, a citizen will receive. It must firstly be noticed that as HDI uses averages for life expectancy and years of education, there is still a problem with distribution. However, the HDI profile gives a more accurate picture of reality. It is almost as simple to use as GDP, but has the benefit of looking at both life expectation and education levels. This is a simple enough measurement, but reveals a huge amount about what is going on "behind the scenes". If citizens are living a long time, it indirectly tells you about crucial factors like pollution, without actually having to measure the pollution rate in a country or city at a given time or location. It is the indirect information that is important. Life expectancy, also, by implication tells you about how much or how little government is spending on health care. A raw figure about years of education is also quite revealing about some issues such as equality of the sexes. If the raw figure is high, it implies strongly that females are being given the

opportunity to become literate, and not only men. So, in conclusion, the HDI approach builds successfully on the older GDP system, to provide a fairly accurate picture of what is going on inside a country, without having to collect data on 20 or 30 different facets of life. The final number for HDI will be between zero and one, with one being the highest and best measure that can be achieved. Thus, a developing economy with low education levels and low life expectancy, might have an HDI of 0.3, for instance Niger, while Norway, with long life expectancy and endless educational chances, together with high income, would have a figure of above 0.9.

MEASURING INEQUALITY

1. We have previously discussed that real GDP per person is not necessarily the best measure of living standards. One reason for this is that incomes are not equally distributed. The Gini coefficient can produce a figure of say 0.9 to indicate that a small group of families control the wealth of an economy, while a figure of 0 would imply complete equality of income distribution.

2. There has been a tendency for income inequality to be growing in countries like the U.S. in recent years, as wealth gets more centralised in the hands of a few. This is a dangerous development, as capitalism has been shown to be destroyable from within. Marx in his mind-bendingly brilliant analysis of the capital machine, argued that the centralisation of wealth in the hands of a few, coupled with the progressive exploitation of the many, would lead to the inevitable end of the capitalist model. It would be naive indeed to think that capitalism is necessarily going to last forever. It is the product of the industrial revolution, and could vanish just as easily as the feudal system or the socialist system. The economist Schumpeter in his masterwork *Capitalism, Socialism and Democracy* (1942), argued that capitalism would shrivel up in a long drawn out metamorphosis into bureaucratic quasi socialism.

3. The battle against income inequality is a battle to conserve the capitalist model, because if Marx is correct, it is inequality based on ruthless exploitation, which poses the greatest risk to the free market system. In order to solve the problem of income inequality, in its extreme, iniquitous form, it is first necessary to have a way of quantifying the problem. The basic way of measuring is provided by the Lorenz curve, and the Gini coefficient is actually based on this. The Lorenz curve sets up a model of perfect equality and shows how the real world may differ from this in a range of countries, by their deviation from the ideal. The 45 degree line on the following diagram illustrates a situation of perfect equality, where everyone has identical income. Then the particular economy one is investigating is superimposed on the model, as a curve moving away from the diagonal. The greater the curve, the greater the inequality. The reason is that the area under the diagonal represents one unit, and the area between the curve and the diagonal is a fraction of the triangle's area. If the curve is very large, then it gives a high percentage of the triangle's area, leading to a value of say 0.8. This figure is actually the Gini coefficient. The reality of such a figure might be something like Saddam Hussein's Iraq, where one family owned most of the assets. If we can measure inequality, then we can try and solve the problem. If we don't try to address this problem, then the dark prophecies written in Karl Marx's *Capital* may eventually come true. In the following diagram, 70% of

the population have to survive on 30% of the cake (GDP).

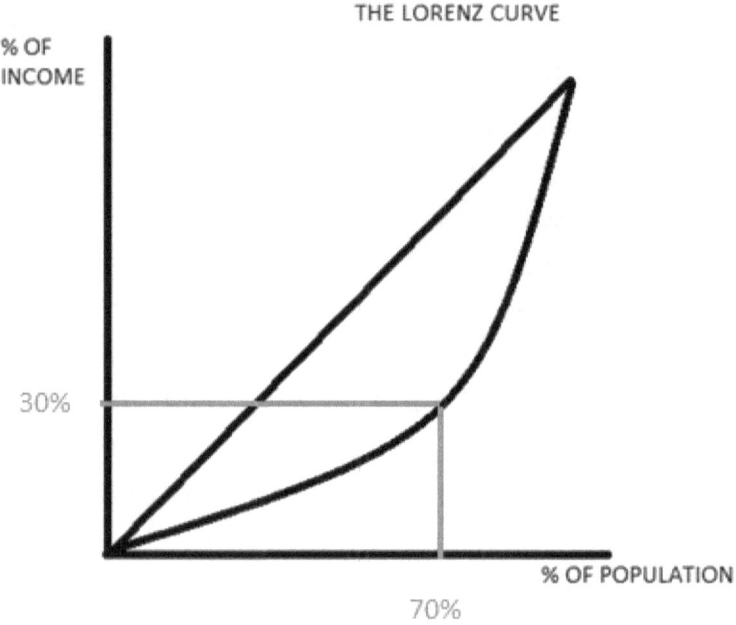

THE LORENZ CURVE

% OF INCOME

30%

% OF POPULATION

70%

KARL MARX

1. It is appropriate to explain and evaluate objectively the views of Karl Marx. His main work was published in 1867 under the title *Capital*. Marx focused on a critique of capitalism, and it links into our discussion of income inequality.

2. Marx argued that the whole course of human history is a dialectical process, of thesis, antithesis and synthesis. The feudal stage was replaced by capitalism, and similarly Marx proposed that capitalism would be replaced by "the dictatorship of the proletariat". The feudal system was displaced by capitalism because the feudal model "put fetters" on enterprise, and these fetters had to be "burst asunder". The feudal model couldn't accommodate the entrepreneur, so the feudal model had to be destroyed in the flurry of the industrial revolution. Marx argued that capitalism would also vanish in the same way, in a final synthesis. We can now examine the details of his argument.

3. He argued that capitalism is fundamentally a system of exploitation, because the profit motive (MR=MC), drives entrepreneurs to exploit workers, paying them as little as possible. There is also a gradual monopolisation of firms, as they strive for higher profit margins, and with this trend, the ability to exploit workers just gets stronger. Workers are made

unemployed by machines, and you end with two polarised groups; a small group of industrialists and a large group of unemployed or exploited workers. This will seal the fate of the capitalist machine, according to the Marxist view. There will be inevitable revolution.

4. The reality in many countries has been rather different, with workers in countries like the US and Europe, gaining in financial power as time has gone on. So it does not seem that the Marxist account of history is entirely accurate. However, the emerging income inequality previously discussed, is somewhat in line with a Marxist view of history. Marx made many other points which ring true. He argued that one reason why capitalism would encounter problems is that to survive it must sell more and more products. However, with workers becoming poorer through the process of exploitation, this would become more and more difficult. We see that capitalism has been very ingenious in getting around this problem. Many workers cannot afford the products of capitalism, but the capitalist financial system has invented the concept of consumer credit, to solve the problem, at least for now. We see debt levels at a personal level, spiralling out of control, and now interest rates are at rock bottom in another attempt by capitalism to facilitate the sale of its product. Even if one rejects the Marxist interpretation of world history, there is no doubt that many of his ideas are intriguing and at least partly true. Before leaving this brief examination of Marx, it is important to mention that the communist experiment

in the Soviet Union, involved the Bolsheviks stealing and adopting the philosophy of Marx. The Soviet model is most likely not the model Marx would have approved of. On the contrary, he envisaged a withering away of the state, rather than the domination of the masses by figures like Stalin. One cannot point to the sometimes unsavoury nature of Soviet communism, as a critique of Marx. The Bolsheviks simply borrowed his ideas to give themselves legitimacy. The only way to justifiable critique Marx, is to read his often profound writings.

TO WHAT EXTENT ARE THE AIMS OF GOVERNMENT IN CONFLICT?

1. We have previously outlined the main aims of government as being such objectives as the reduction of unemployment, the promotion of economic growth, the avoidance of high inflation or deflation, the promotion of a balance of payments surplus, the maintenance of a strong and stable currency, avoiding an excessive budget deficit, and the solution to market failures such as pollution and income inequality. We have also examined the main tools available to government to solve economic problems, namely fiscal, monetary and supply side policy. We can now put these ideas together and explore the extent to which the aims of government are in conflict.

2. One of the main aims is to reduce unemployment. In order to do this, government may increase spending, cut taxes, run a deficit on the budget, cut interest rates and employ quantitative easing. All of these approaches will increase aggregate demand in the economy. Looking at the Keynesian derived formula D=C+I+G+(X-M), we see that lower taxes and interest rates will promote consumption and investment, while spending on public works will increase the value of G. Low interest rates will also cause the exchange rate to depreciate, making exports cheaper, while stopping unnecessary imports. All these factors will cause the

aggregate demand curve to shift to the right. The effect of this should be job creation and economic growth.

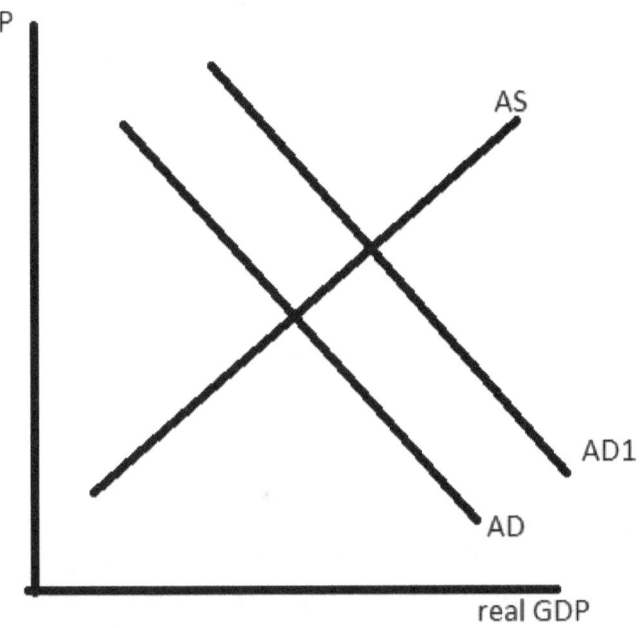

3. If we observe the above diagram with care, we can see a problem. While GDP is rising, and the aim of creating jobs is accomplished, the price level is rising due to the extra demand. So the aim of lower unemployment is somewhat in conflict with the aim of low inflation. This conflict was developed by the economist Phillips, who produced the noted Phillips curve to illustrate the problem in more depth and detail.

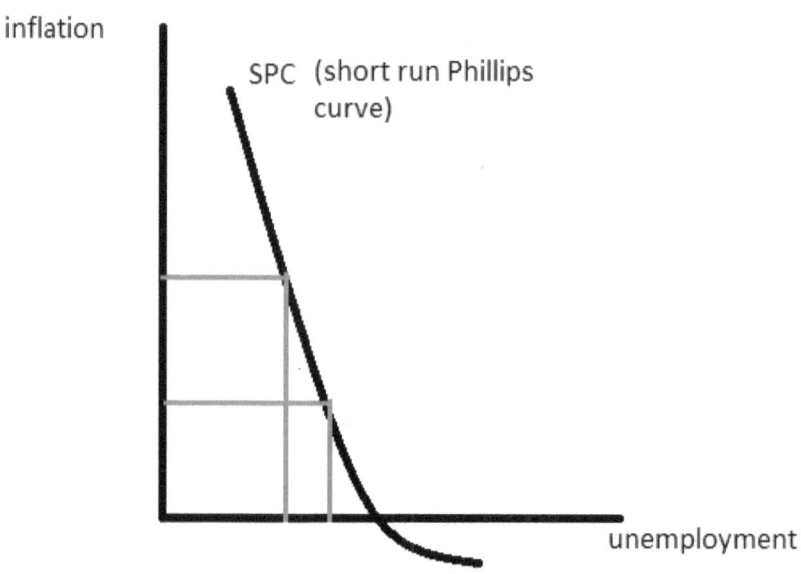

inflation

SPC (short run Phillips curve)

unemployment

4. We can see from the Phillips curve, that as unemployment is reduced, this causes inflationary pressure; prices start rising too fast. The reason is twofold. As workers get jobs, perhaps through public works projects, they spend more money, and so aggregate demand rises, and with it inflationary pressure. This is demand-pull inflation. However there is another reason, to be found in the fact that as skilled workers become rarer and rarer, firms must pay them higher wages, and this causes their costs to rise. This is called cost-push inflation. We can also observe, that when unemployment becomes very high, inflation turns negative, and this is the spectre of deflation (falling prices).

5. The conflict between the aims of lower unemployment and lower inflation represent one of the main conflicts of government objectives. However, there are several other clear conflicts, which lead one to the conclusion that a politician's life is not an easy one. If the government of China wants to create fast growth, this will cause excess pollution and market failure. The reason is that the fastest short term growth comes from unregulated industrial production; not putting a cap on pollution emission levels. There is also a conflict between reducing unemployment through a Keynesian strategy, and keeping the budget deficit under control. A further conflict is seen in the notion that encouraging exports may eventually cause the currency to become too strong. Yet not all aims are in conflict. For example the aims of growth and job creation are in harmony.

THE LONG RUN PHILLIPS CURVE

1. The long run Phillips curve shows that sometimes the aims of government are in such radical conflict that trying to achieve one aim, may make it impossible to achieve another aim, and the initial aim will also be damaged. The long run Phillips curve, also called the expectations augmented Phillips curve, was created by the economists Friedman and Phelps. They designed the enterprise to show that Keynesian demand management could be terribly counterproductive. The curve shows that if government throws money at the economic problem of rising unemployment, through the method of public works projects, then in the short run, jobs will undoubtedly be created. One example would be the jobs created in the US when the giant Hoover dam was constructed. However, Friedman and Phelps argue that the benefits would only be available in the short term. In the longer term, the inflationary pressure created by this somewhat artificial public works job creation process, would cause firms to be forced to grant higher wages, and this would cause job losses. At the end of the day you would be left with the same basic level of unemployment as before, but with higher inflation. One key to understanding this curve, is the idea of expectations. Workers are seen as highly intelligent and they will expect higher inflation from the artificiality of the public works process, and they will thus demand higher wages, causing the whole

Keynesian project to crumble into dust. It must be remembered that one of the driving motivations of Friedman and the Chicago school was to minimise the role of government in markets; small government rather than large. The long run Phillips curve is an attempt to say that governments cannot choose a Phillips curve trade-off between unemployment and inflation, where the former is say 5% and the latter 2%. Friedman is trying to prove that such a trade-off is not possible, and that government has less power and capacity than it would like to think. This gets back to the idea that markets should be generally left alone, and attempts at demand management and central planning are destined to end in failure.

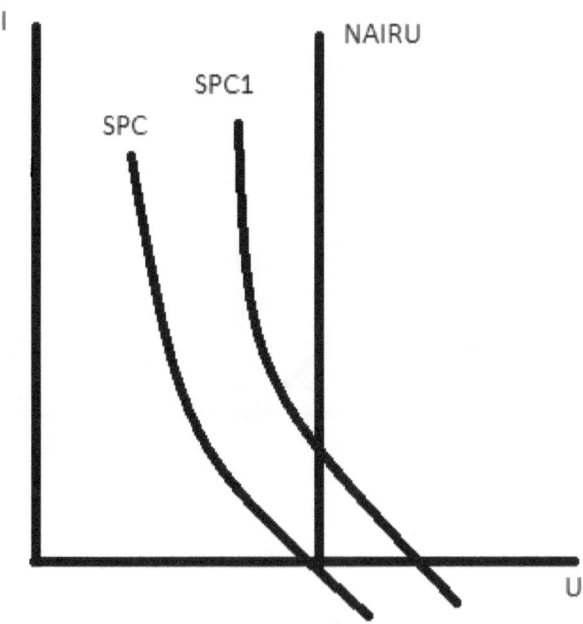

2. The above diagram might seem difficult to interpret at first glance, but a step by step examination should clarify. If government spends more money, unemployment will fall. This will create inflationary pressure and wage demands. Firms will then cut the number of workers and you end with the same level of joblessness as before, but with higher inflation. This is a lose-lose situation, where even the initial aim of job creation is lost. We can label the three stages A, B, and C and this should clarify the situation.

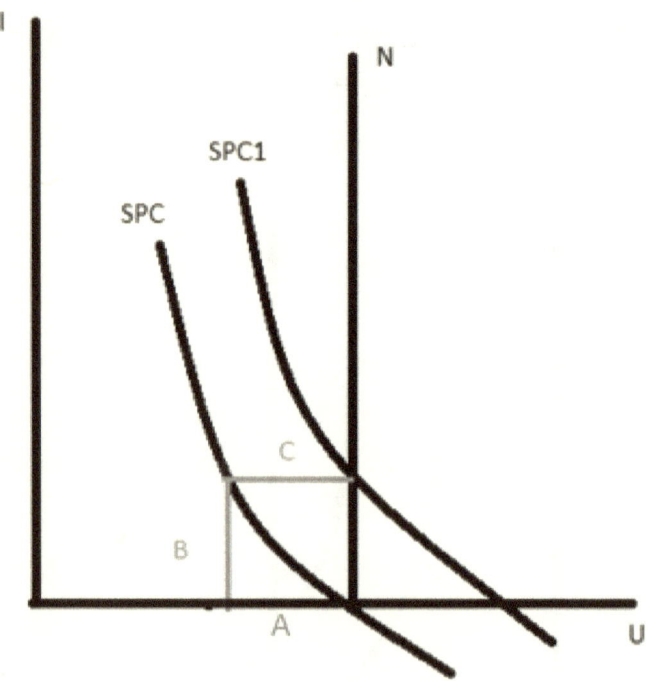

3. The labels on these diagrams also require a small amount of explanation. SPC is the short run Phillips curve as before, however N stands for the natural rate of unemployment, while NAIRU (an alternative label) is the non-accelerating inflation rate of unemployment. What is meant by this is the proposition that there is a so called natural rate of unemployment in any economy at any given time, and any attempt to manipulate this by higher levels of government spending will simply be inflationary. The only way to reduce the natural rate of unemployment is by improving the efficiency of the economy (supply side measures) or by careful use of monetary policy.

SHORT RUN AND LONG RUN AGGREGATE DEMAND AND SUPPLY CURVES

1. In the short run there is a measure of agreement that we have a standard total demand and total supply curve, which sets up a nation's equilibrium. If changes are made to say interest rates, then this will have an impact on both demand and supply. Lower interest rates will cause aggregate demand to rise, due to increased consumption, investment and exports, and aggregate supply to also rise a little due to lower firms borrowing costs. We see on the diagram growth and inflationary pressure on the demand side, together with some supply side growth and a lessening of inflationary pressure. The outcome might be growth and some inflationary tendencies.

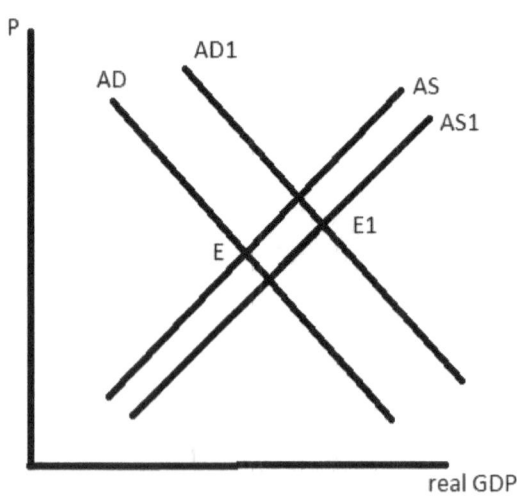

2. While there is some measure of general agreement about the above short run scenario, in the long run, there is little true consensus. The Keynesian camp are of the view that there will be little inflation if there is high unemployment, and so their version of the aggregate supply curve is basically horizontal, until unemployment is very low (full employment). Terms like the natural rate of unemployment, or full employment, are deliberately vague and imprecise. Full employment might simply mean very low unemployment, or it might signify that the number of vacancies is equal to the number of job seekers. The Keynesian long run AD, AS curve looks like this.

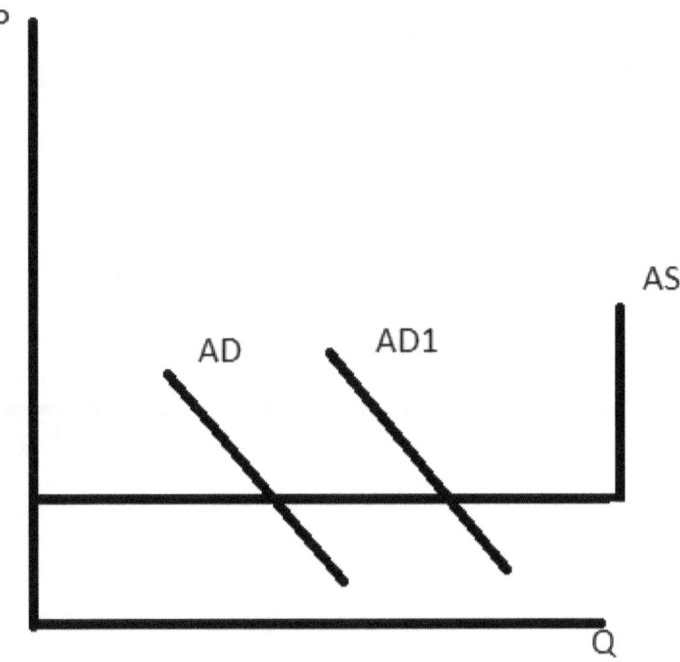

3. The neo-classical school of economists would hotly disagree with the Keynesian long run curve. The reason is that the long run Phillips curve suggests that inflation is very likely if Keynesian strategies are adopted. Accordingly, the neo-classical supply curve is vertical, showing an economy at full capacity. It is no accident that they argued for a curve diametrically opposed to the Keynesian vision.

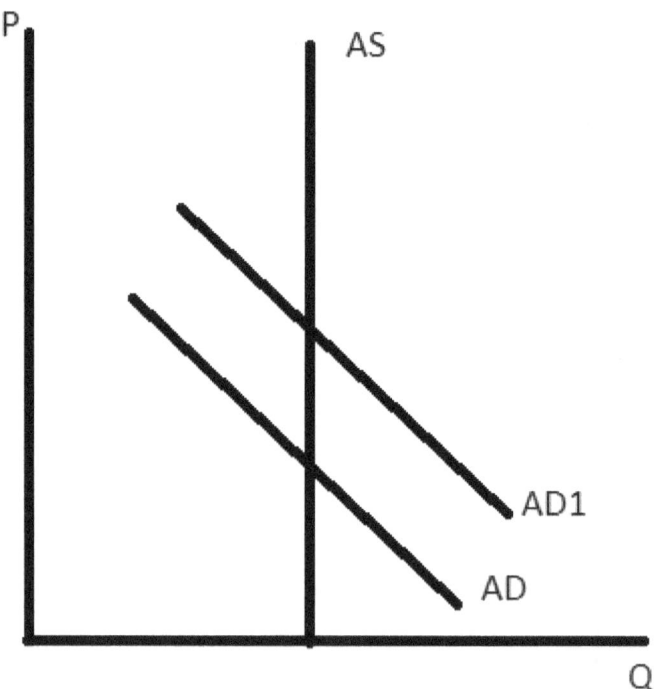

4. One can develop the above curve scenario further. If there is the successful implementation of supply side policies, this will cause the AS curve to shift right, delivering the twin benefits of economic growth and lower inflation. Correct use of monetary policy would have a similar outcome, according the Friedman's analysis.

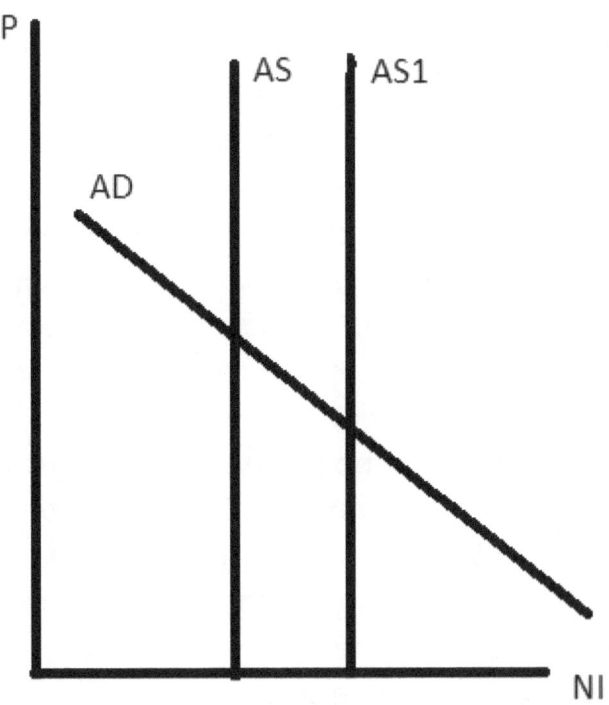

THE TAX SYSTEM

1. An examination of macroeconomics requires some explanation of the tax system. Taxes are split into direct taxes such as income tax and corporation tax, and indirect tax which is tax on goods and services.

2. Taxes like income tax are called direct, because the money is taken directly from the worker on a pay–as-you-earn basis. Each month his wage will be net of tax, meaning after deduction of tax. Taxes like income tax can be proportional, progressive or regressive. A proportional tax is where every earner pays say 20% of their earnings in taxation, irrespective of how high of low their salary. This means that a high income earner will pay more tax in money terms than a low income earner. Progressive tax is where there are several tax bands, and the high income earner will pay a higher percentage of his income in taxation. For instance if he earns £100,000, the first £20,000 might be taxed at 15%, the next £50,000 at 30% and the final £30,000 as 45%. The final possibility is so named regressive tax, because a low income earner will pay a higher percentage of his income in taxation. This might seem unusual, but one way of attracting business investment into an area is to offer tax breaks. Some Cantons in Switzerland will have a standard rate on incomes up to say 100,000 CHF, but a lower rate on income above this limit. A wealthy person will still pay more tax in money

terms, but it will be less as a percentage of his total income.

3. There is much debate presently about the efficacy of progressive tax versus proportional. It is felt that progressive tax causes tax evasion, a brain drain and creates a disincentive to enterprise. Antagonists to this view point to the lack of equity involved in people earning huge sums and paying no more in tax percentage than a low income worker. They argue that the extra tax revenue is needed to provide extra merit goods to disadvantaged citizens. It is, however, far from clear that progressive tax always yields more tax revenue, and in this regard the Laffer curve has already been discussed.

4. Indirect tax on alcohol, tobacco and gasoline has long been considered regressive, because it consumes a higher percentage of a poor person's wage, than of a rich man's earnings. The poor are more likely to be addicted due to lack of education and few other relaxations from the stress of life. As there are many more poor people than wealthy, the burden of tax on demerit goods is paid more by the poor than the rich. Tax on demerit goods is called specific unit tax, for example £3 on a bottle of alcohol. The supply curve shifts to the left to show the unit tax. This was examined in an earlier chapter. There is another form of indirect taxation called ad valorem or percentage tax. This would be, for example, a sales tax of 15%. If a consumer buys an expensive car, the amount of money

paid in tax would be much more than on a cheap car, so the supply curve shifts in a non-parallel manner to indicate this. The supply curve is used to show the taxation of goods and services, because effectively the firm's costs rise, as they must pay the tax to the government. As mentioned previously, the firm will try hard to pass the tax burden onto the consumer, but this is only fully possible with inelastic demerit goods, or highly desired brands.

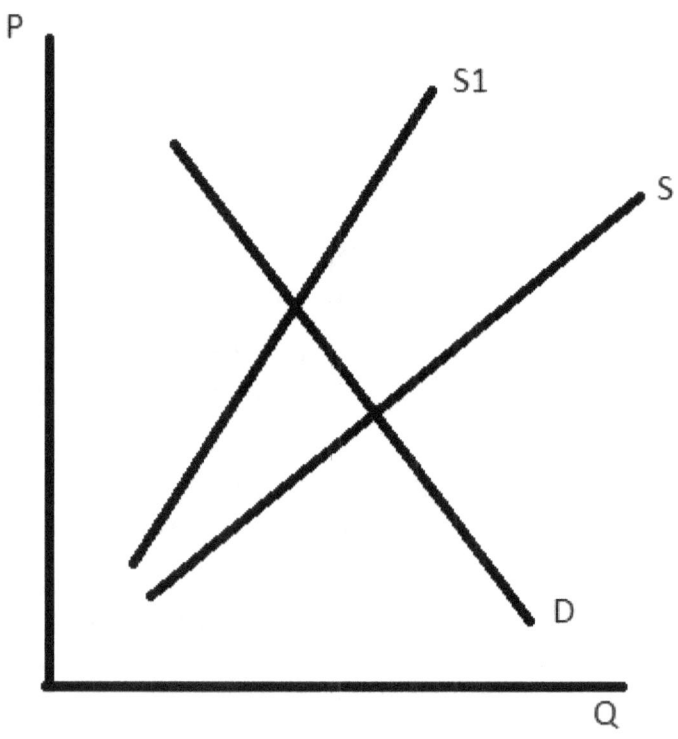

THE BALANCE OF PAYMENTS

1. The balance of payments is made up of the current account and the capital account. The current account relates to exports and imports, while the capital account (sometimes named the financial account), relates to the items hot money, bonds and shares, and foreign direct investment.

2. Let us first focus on the current account. The current account covers exports and imports of primary, secondary and tertiary products. If a country exports more than it imports, in terms of value or revenue (not quantity), this creates a current account surplus. A deficit on the current account is when the value of exports is less than the value of imports. Primary goods are products like gold, copper and corn, secondary goods are "made" goods like computers and motor vehicles, and tertiary goods are services like tourism or education. Some economies are famous for their exports, for example Swiss watches, German cars, or Japanese electronics. These countries have a current account surplus and this is an overall injection into the circular flow, creating economic growth. The most recent annual current account surplus for Germany is around $285bn.

3. Countries with a continuous deficit will eventually experience economic contraction, ceteris paribus. The

US is noted for its persistent deficit on the current account. An ongoing deficit on the current account represents a continuous leakage from the circular flow, and will slow growth and promote recession. An accompanying problem is the fact that as a country imports more than it exports, the exchange rate loses value, making imports very costly. The US avoids this problem, because money flows into the capital account, keeping the currency strong. This is because the dollar is an attractive investment currency, as it is attached to the world's most powerful economy, backed by military might.

4. The current account also includes a number of minor factors such as foreign aid payments, remittances back to family from overseas workers, and net property income from abroad (profits from overseas investments).

5. The capital account relates to hot money, which is cash floating around the globe looking for the best return and the safest investment. If the interest rate in say China is 7%, but in the US it is 2%, many investors will consider investing in China, so long as they feel the investment is secure. It is not enough to offer a high interest rate, safety is a prime issue also. An investment in Russia or Argentina might not be so wise, given the fact that both countries have defaulted on their debt obligations in fairly recent years.

6. Another facet of the capital account is bonds and shares. If money pours into the US from China, in the form of the Chinese government buying US government bonds, this inflow is a positive figure on the US capital account. The inflow also strengthens the dollar, as the dollar is being purchased as part of the transaction.

7. The last facet of the capital account is foreign direct investment. This is where, for example, a Chinese millionaire invests in a business project in Los Angeles. This involves risk and long term commitment. This is the opposite of hot money, which can often be transferred at the push of a button from one country to another.

8. So we have an overview of the balance of payments. If export revenue exceeds spending on imports, this gives a current account surplus, while a deficit on the current account is created when a country's export revenue is less than spending on imports. A surplus on the current account of the balance of payments is an injection into the circular flow, and it promotes growth and creates jobs. A surplus also makes the currency stronger, because when overseas consumers buy a country's exports, they have to buy the currency first. The capital account has a positive inflow, when hot money flows into a country's banks, seeking high safe interest, or where an overseas investor buys shares in a company in a country, or where an overseas investor invests directly in a business start-up or project. The positive inflows create growth and make the exchange rate

stronger. Of special significance is exports and imports, as this represents reality. Hot money can vanish in an instant, at the press of a computer key, but someone buying a German car in Hong Kong, means real export revenue for Germany, and a job for a German worker. Money flowing in through the capital account is available for lending inside the country, and this can facilitate low interest loans which enhance consumption and investment.

EXCHANGE RATES

1. The exchange rate is the rate at which one currency swaps or exchanges against another. For example, there might be 2CHF to £1. Exchange rates are usually floating or flexible, meaning that the value depends on demand and supply. The dollar would become stronger or weaker, depending on how much export revenue or spending on imports the country has. A deficit on the current account will gradually weaken the exchange rate. The reason is simply that to buy a Japanese car in the US, you must also buy the Japanese currency, and sell the US currency, at some stage in the purchasing process. This means that as you buy the product of another economy, you automatically make their currency stronger, while weakening your own economy's exchange rate. The exchange rate depends largely on exports and imports, with a surplus making the exchange rate stronger, however speculative purchasing is also important. The foreign exchange markets are involved in a lot of speculative trading. Basically a currency will be bought if it is expected to rise in value, and the very purchase will help the process. This is a form of wish fulfilment. The transactions on the capital account, whether it is a purchase of bonds or shares or FDI are also important. Every inflow makes the currency stronger, because at some stage in the process, the inflow involves a selling of one currency and a purchase of another. If I decide

to buy a business in Chile, while having my purchasing power in sterling, I must sell sterling and buy the Chilean currency, thus strengthening it.

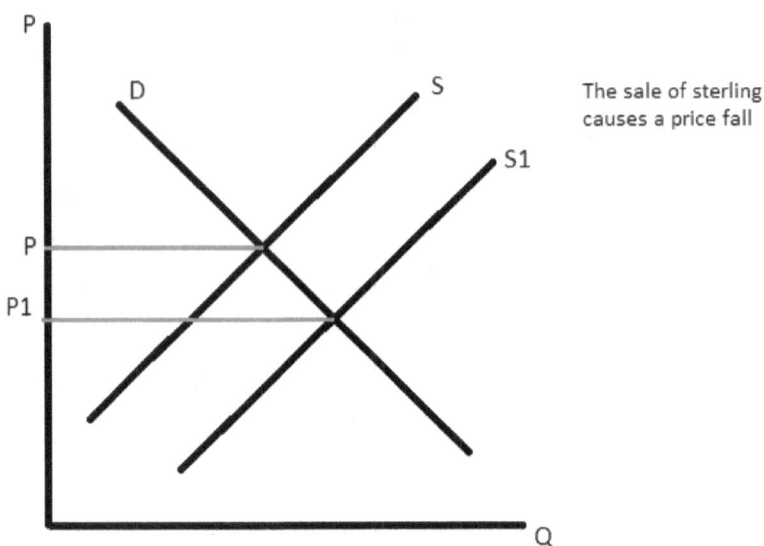

The sale of sterling causes a price fall

2. Exchange rates are mostly floating, but occasionally they are fixed. For instance, the Saudi currency and the Hong Kong currency are pegged to the dollar. A fixed exchange rate is normally for political reasons, because oil is so important to the US it is denominated in dollars, or Hong Kong wishes to express its separateness from the Chinese regime. One problem with a fixed exchange rate is that it creates distortions in the balance of payments. If a country imports too much using a floating exchange rate, the excessive importation will weaken the currency, effectively putting a break on imports. A fixed exchange rate economy has no such problem, it can import to excess,

and the currency will not depreciate. Argentina experienced this problem. Ultimately it leads to an unsustainable situation and an economic collapse. A floating exchange rate has the advantage of an automatic stabiliser. The more a country imports, the weaker the currency becomes, thus stopping unnecessary imports, while simultaneously facilitating cheaper exports. Another problem with a fixed exchange rate is that often interest rates have to be held high, as they are used to maintain the strength of the currency. This can cause a recession, as was the case in Hong Kong in 1998, when interest rates went into double figures.

3. A managed exchange rate is somewhere between fixed and flexible. In practice, many economies have a managed exchange rate, in that the central bank and government will be acutely aware that the value of the currency has an impact on the price of exports and imports, and ultimately on the current account. Comments have been made on the fact that the Chinese government has been manipulating or managing its currency excessively over recent years, in order to keep the price of their exports cheap, especially to the US. Another example of a managed currency would be the recent Swiss experiment when they pegged the Swiss franc to the euro at an exchange rate of 1.2 CHF to 1 euro. This experiment was designed to keep the price of exports from Switzerland to euroland low, but it involved the Swiss central bank buying a huge amount of euros, to keep the franc low. The experiment ended recently, partly due to the fact that the Swiss central bank has a

deep belief in free markets, partly because some recovering markets could afford the higher prices, and partly because the weakness of the euro was not expected to end in the foreseeable future.

THE MARSHALL LERNER CONDITION

1. The Marshall Lerner condition is important when one considers the relationship between exports, imports, elasticity and the current account. The central idea is quite simple; if the combined elasticity of exports and imports is greater than 1, then a depreciation of the exchange rate will improve the balance of payments on current account.

2. If we consider a more developed country like the US, Switzerland, the UK, or Japan, these economies tend to export mostly elastic branded goods. They are mostly focused on products we want but don't necessarily need, such as deluxe watches or expensive cars. There are many competing brands available from other countries; Germany even competes with Switzerland in the sphere of luxury watches. All these products benefit from a depreciation of the exchange rate. If the Swiss franc loses value, it simply means that a watch exported to Canada or the Seychelles costs less. This means that a depreciation of the currency will prima facie improve the current account of a developed, brand selling nation. Most advanced democracies fall into the category, as they specialise in manufactured products and services, rather than primary goods.

3. In addition to looking at exports, it is also important to cast a glance at imports. If imports are also elastic, then a country with a depreciating exchange rate will reduce unneeded luxury imports. If the imports are mostly essentials like oil or wheat, then they must still be imported in spite of a weaker currency.

4. Putting these ideas together, if the combined elasticity of exports and imports is elastic and more than one, then a devaluation or depreciation will improve the current account.

5. If an economy exports mostly inelastic goods like gold, tin and gas, then a depreciation will simply weaken the current account. The main reason is that a fall in the price of the export will only slightly increase sales, because of the inelastic demand curve, previously investigated in microeconomics. So economies like Saudi Arabia or Russia would not benefit from a depreciation, as this would reduce export revenue, and damage the current account.

6. An economy like China is worth special mention as it is largely an exporter of manufactured goods. This means that it benefits from a depreciation, and this might explain why the Chinese government endeavours to keep its currency low against other world currencies like the dollar. As its exports cheapen, the export revenue rises, as we are dealing with an elastic demand curve, with a PED of more than one.

7. In conclusion, if we observe a MDC like France or Germany or Japan, a slight fall in the value of the exchange rate, called a depreciation or, if deliberate, a devaluation, will make exports cheaper and as the exports are mostly elastic, the export revenue will rise. So long as imports are also elastic, the devaluation will help the current account. Specifically, the combined PED of exports and imports must exceed one for a devaluation to automatically improve the current account.

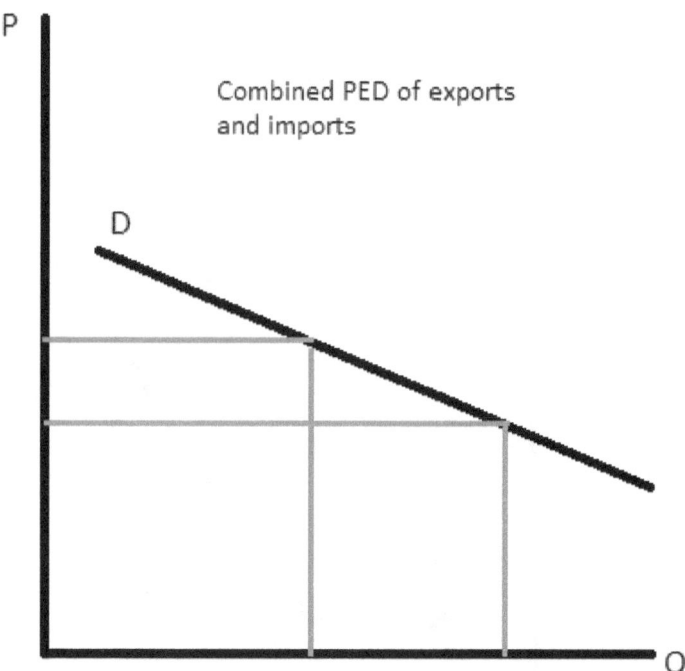

8. It should be realised that a depreciation of the exchange rate will not immediately improve the current account, where the combined PED of exports and imports satisfies the Marshall Lerner condition. The advantages of the lower exchange rate might take some time to permeate through the trading system. The main reason is that old contracts have to be honoured at old prices, and older stock needs to be sold off, before new stocks are bought at a cheaper price. So a UK importer of Japanese motorbikes will only be able to take advantage of a lower yen, when he enters into a new contract for additional supply. This idea is often represented by the J curve, which shows that a depreciation may result in a short term worsening of the current account, before an improvement sets in.

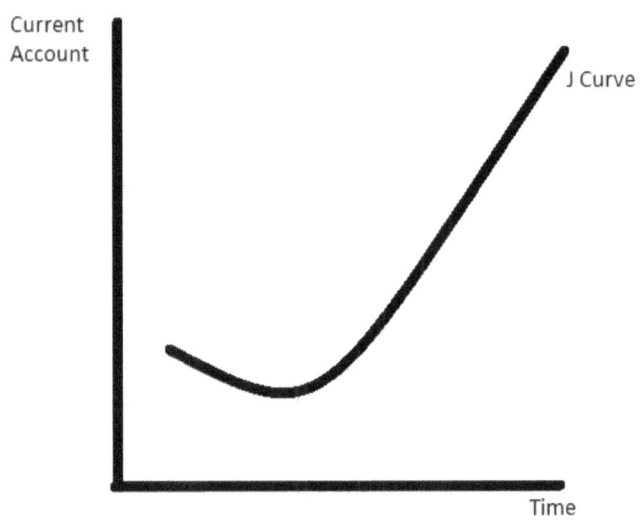

FREE TRADE

1. There has long been a debate about whether it is better to run a country based on free trade, or on the competing thesis of protectionism. Free trade has a whole range of very profound advantages, and we can now enumerate these. Free trade implies that there are no barriers to export and import, such as tariffs, quotas or subsidies.

2. Free trade allows for a great increase in the level of competition. This means that prices fall, and quality and choice rises, as there is a move towards allocative efficiency. The consumer gains sovereignty and power. There is also increased productive efficiency, leading to stronger growth, with lower inflation. The benefits associated with perfect competition flow into a free trade environment. The following diagram shows that competition creates growth through the supply side of falling AC.

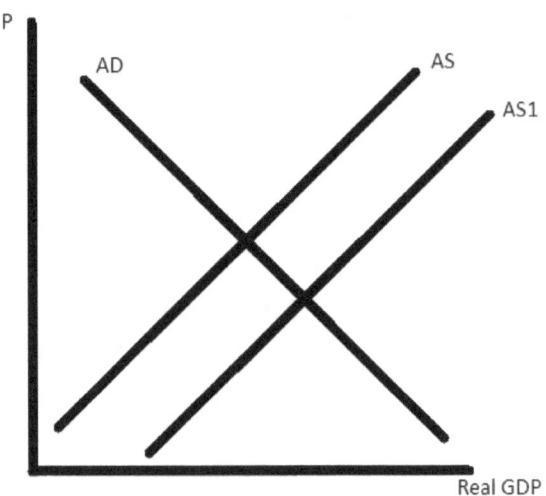

3. A free trade environment has a lot of positive advantages because it means that subsidies tend to be reduced or eliminated. Subsidies are designed often to keep imports out, but they are very costly to the taxpayer and have a huge opportunity cost. The tax revenue could be spent on schools and hospitals, rather than being given to highly inefficient farmers.

4. A free trade environment allows each country to focus on what they are good at, for example Switzerland has an advantage in ski holidays and watches, while Jamaica has an advantage in bananas and beach vacations. It would be virtually insane for the UK to focus on growing bananas, because Jamaica has a climate advantage. In Economics this is the concept of comparative advantage, introduced by the famous economist David Ricardo. Ricardo made his fortune on the financial markets, before turning to politics and

writing. His famed work has the unexciting title *On the Principles of Political Economy and Taxation* (1817), but the concept of comparative advantage is profound indeed. The idea is that countries do best to focus on those products where they have a comparative advantage, meaning where they can produce the product at lowest opportunity cost. The key idea here is that countries must produce products where they have lowest opportunity cost. Opportunity cost is different from lowest average cost, which is called absolute advantage. Absolute advantage is another reason for specialising on a few select products or services, but comparative advantage is opportunity cost based.

5. The notion of comparative advantage can easily be outlined. If we consider the following diagram, we can see that Germany can produce 100 cars for the lost opportunity of 5000 tonnes of bananas, while Jamaica could also produce 100 cars, but the lost opportunity in terms of banana production would be much greater, say 50000 tonnes. Thus, Germany should focus all its resources on car production, and specialise in this area, while Jamaica should focus on bananas. Germany will then import bananas as needed from Jamaica, and Jamaica can purchase cars from Germany. The overall outcome will be a world increase in both banana and or car production. We can explore this by considering the two scenarios below. In the top table Germany tries to produce both cars and bananas, and Jamaica ditto. On the bottom there is specialisation in accordance with Ricardo's concept of comparative advantage. The world

output increases if comparative advantage is employed, and this is one of the strongest arguments in favour of free trade.

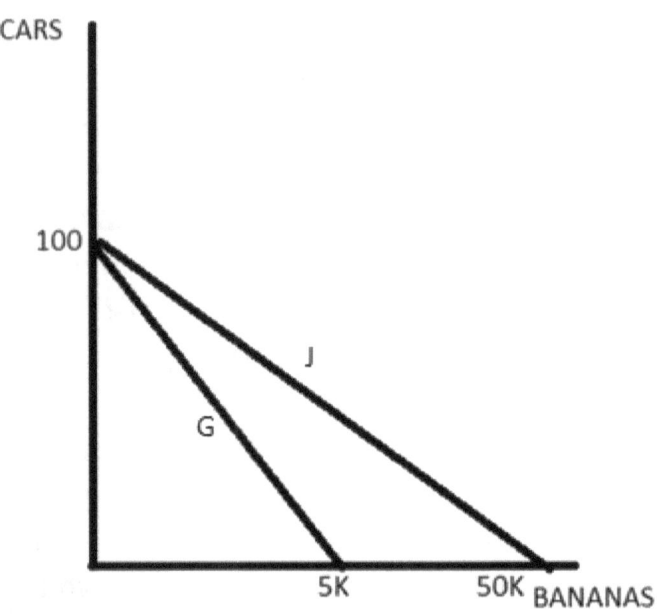

WITHOUT FREE TRADE

CARS	BANANAS	
100	5000	Germany
100	50000	Jamaica
200	55000	Total

WITH FREE TRADE

CARS	BANANAS	
200	0	G
0	100,000	J
200	100,000	T

6. There are many other arguments in favour of free trade. One is that free trade avoids the inflation generating effects of tariffs and quotas. A tariff is a tax on imports, and one effect is that it causes prices for the consumer to rise. A quota is a number or value limit, and this has a similar effect. The price rises can be easily identified on the following diagrams, which will be more fully explained in the next chapter.

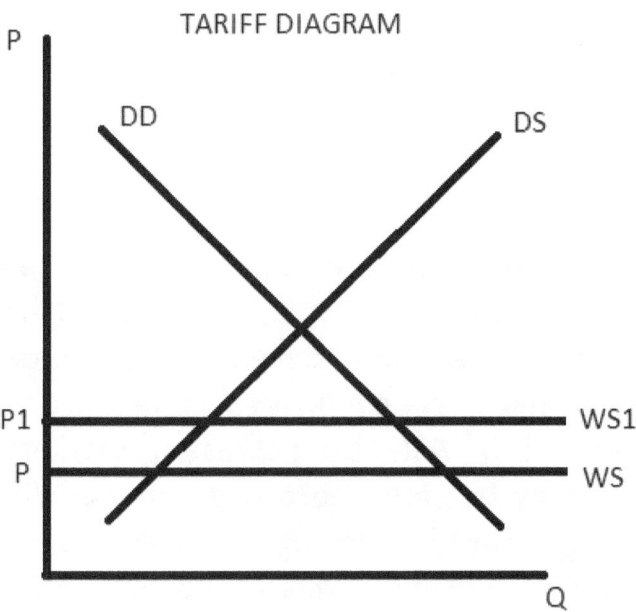

TARIFF DIAGRAM

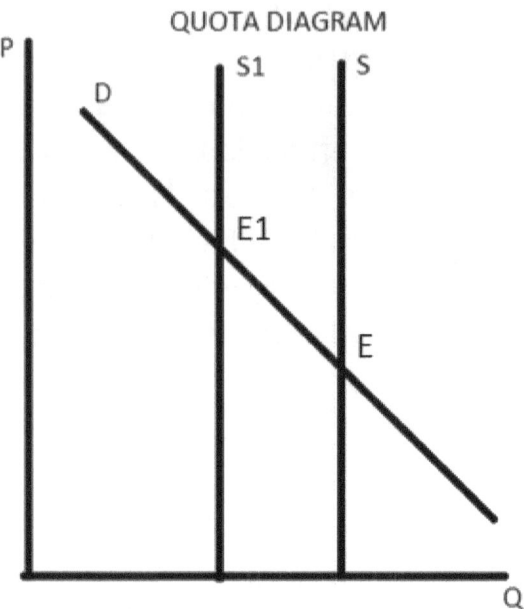

QUOTA DIAGRAM

7. A great advantage of free trade is that it gives less prosperous nations, called less developed countries, the chance to grow and develop through exporting. This means that these countries will be more politically stable, and they will also represent markets in the future, as they become more prosperous. Who would have thought thirty years ago that one of the main markets for European luxuries would now be China?

8. A world based on the free trade model enhances democracy, because it is not just products which get exported, it is values and ideas too.

9. Free trade allows for the free flow of capital, which allows for investment in overseas stock markets, and in foreign direct investment.

PROTECTIONISM

1. Protectionism is a world where individual countries put up barriers to trade. The motive is often to save domestic jobs. For instance, the US may put a barrier up, to stop the importation of cotton from Africa, or steel from Korea. The obvious rationale is that if these goods are made inside the US, rather than imported, then domestic employment will be protected. Another benefit is that tariffs may yield some tax revenue. The tax revenue from tariffs is shown below. The tariff diagram appears complex, but it is not actually so. The demand and supply curves look at domestic demand and supply, while the world supply line is superimposed on this. The WS1 line is the supply curve after the imposition of the indirect tax. The main effects are rising prices, a fall in imports and an expansion of domestic employment. There is also tax revenue. As we observe the diagram, the box Tax is the tax revenue, while the move from 1,2 to 3,4 shows the fall in imports, and the lines a,b to c,d show the increase in the quantity of jobs inside the country; domestic jobs. Equilibrium is where DD meets WS, before the tax, and where DD meets WS1 after the imposed tax.

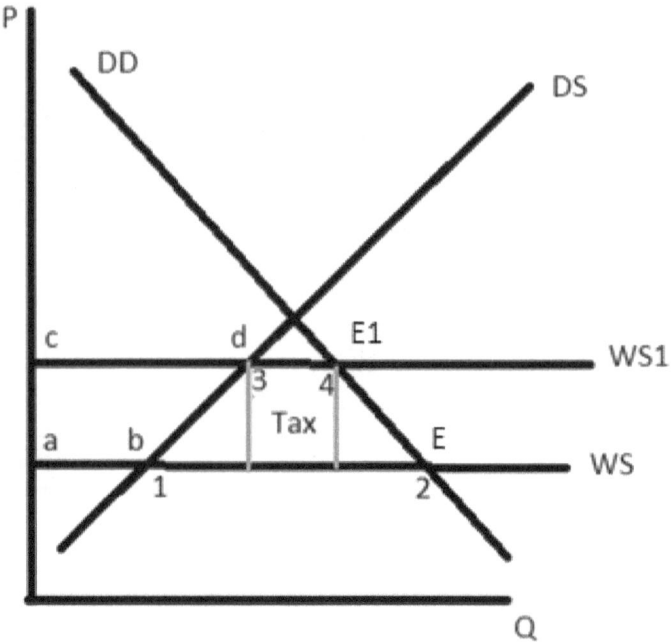

2. There are other arguments in favour of a protectionist model. One is that new enterprises, called sunrise industries, need to be allowed to develop and grow up behind protecting barriers, until they are strong enough to weather world competition. A similar argument can be advanced for old sunset industries.

3. Arguments can also be made against the dumping of cheap exports from other countries. Sometimes these products may be exported below production cost, perhaps with the help of a government subsidy, in order to penetrate markets. China has often been accused of dumping.

4. If there is protectionism it may stop the risk of capital flight, where vast sums of hot money can leave a country overnight, if there is a threatening economic crisis. This often precipitates the feared crisis.

5. A final protectionist argument is that a country might need to be relatively self-sufficient, especially in food production. This argument is certainly strong in times of war, for example Switzerland in the middle of war-torn Europe in the early 1940s.

THE PROBLEMS OF LESS DEVELOPED COUNTRIES AND THEIR SOLUTION

1. Less developed countries (LDCs) experience a range of problems. They may not implement fiscal policy, monetary policy and supply side policy in the optimum way. There may be gross income and wealth inequality, over-reliance on primary commodities, corruption, low education levels, racism and religious intolerance, illiteracy, infectious disease, poor infrastructure, lack of merit goods and public goods. Management may be based on outmoded values of age precedence, and females may be relegated to a situation of inequality, akin to being treated like property.

2. The human development index of LDCs will normally be a low value, reflecting very low real GDP per capita at PPP. HDI has a minimum of 0 and a maximum of 1, and figures around 0.3 are not uncommon. A low HDI means not only lack of income, it means very low life expectancy, and little education. It is quite common for life expectancy in some African and Asian countries to average less than 50 years, while in more developed countries (MDCs) it can be over 80 years.

3. In addition to a poor HDI figure, the Gini coefficient will usually also be a worrying statistic, for example 0.7 where there is gross income inequality, with most of the population having to survive on a small percentage

of the nation's output. This is akin to a family of five having a quarter of the pizza between them, while the rich man has three quarters to himself.

4. One particular problem which must be mentioned, is over-reliance on one or more primary commodities. Often an LDC will produce one or two basic agricultural or mineral products. Primary commodities are very price volatile, due to being highly inelastic in terms of both demand and supply. When the price fluctuates downward, which can be caused by rising supply or falling demand, this often has a drastic effect on the income of the farmer and his family. A relatively small fall in demand or rise in supply can have an exaggerated effect on price. Similarly, it impacts on tax revenue and government spending. Volatility makes financial planning difficult. One year there will be enough tax revenue to finance education, next year the primary school will be closed due to lack of funds. Due to low education levels, workers in LDCs are often trapped in primary production. The fall in export revenue due to an increase in supply of a product like tea, is detailed below.

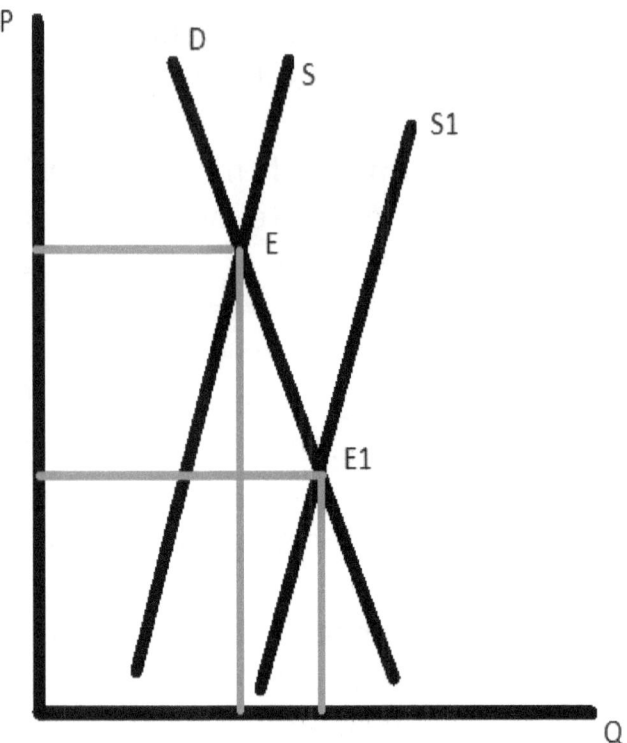

5. The problems of LDCs are deep rooted and not easy to solve. There are two approaches to their solution. One is to emphasise aid. The economist Sachs in his book *The End of Poverty* (2005) argues that the present aid budget of $50bn a year is woefully inadequate, and that rich nations should give 1% of GDP in foreign aid, which would propel the aid figure to nearer $200bn a year. The aid budget could be spent on infrastructure and merit goods such as schools and hospitals. With 1m people a year still perishing from malaria, there is clearly much to be done. Critics of this approach believe that aid just makes people lazy and dependent. They

point to the fact that countries receiving the most aid, are still amongst the poorest. It removes the incentive for industry, if there is a free handout. Also aid can be seen as encouraging corruption and even fermenting civil war. The reason is that aid money gives the incentive for theft. Fighting over ownership of a foreign aid budget is arguably as common as fighting over diamond or copper reserves. Writers like Moyo in her book *Dead Aid* (2009), suggest that it is much better to develop through free trade. She emphasises the fact that wealthy countries should reduce or eliminate their protectionist barriers, such as tariffs, quotas and subsidies. Subsidies in the developed world to farmers are circa $1bn a day. The removal of these barriers would allow exportation from LDCs to MDCs on an enhanced scale, allowing growth and prosperity in poor countries through current account surpluses. It does not seem unreasonable to suggest that a combination of aid and trade might be best. A country cannot trade if it does not have an infrastructure of ports, airports and production and freezing facilities. There can also be no business without a legal system that will impartially enforce contracts.

6. There is a subtle difference between development and growth. Growth simply means rising GDP, but development focuses on the broader perspective offered by the Human Development Index, of incomes, education and life expectancy.

7. The main aid agencies are the World Bank and the International Monetary Fund. The former lends money at a low rate of interest for long term infrastructure projects, while the IMF is more of a fire brigade, offering emergency loans when a country cannot afford imports. There has been a lot of criticism of both "aid" organisations, on the ground that they seem to be agents of the rich and powerful nations. Often as a condition of aid, an LDC will be required to remove its protectionist barriers, however the wealthy economies of the EU, US and Japan, refuse to reciprocate. This has led to what can only be called an uneven playing field. The IMF in particular has come in for scathing criticism, because of its insistence that countries in need, such as Jamaica, undergo a structural adjustment programme, as a precondition of getting a loan. This means getting rid of protectionism, and running a budget surplus. In the case of Jamaica this has led to the virtual destruction of domestic farming, and a lot of hardship through cuts in government spending. The loans from the IMF and World Bank, often become shackles which indebt poor nations into the future. The so called aid agency becomes the cause of the problem, rather than the solution. The DVD *Life and Debt* (2003), gives an excellent example of how the aid agencies do not always make the problem better. They are often seen as mere agents of the US and the EU. The IMF forced Jamaica to eliminate protectionist barriers to agriculture, and this has led to imports flowing one way, from the US to Jamaica, causing the destruction of a once flourishing farming industry.